CREAT

Macaron Basics

an illustrated step-by-step guide

Tan Phay Shing

Marshall Cavendish Cuisine

Editor: Lydia Leong
Designer: Benson Tan
All photos by Hongde Photography except step-by-step photos by Tan Phay Shing

Published by Marshall Cavendish Cuisine
An imprint of Marshall Cavendish International

A member of the
Times Publishing Group

Other Marshall Cavendish Offices:
Marshall Cavendish Corporation. 99 White Plains Road, Tarrytown NY 10591-9001, USA • Marshall Cavendish International (Thailand) Co Ltd. 253 Asoke, 12th Flr, Sukhumvit 21 Road, Klongtoey Nua, Wattana, Bangkok 10110, Thailand • Marshall Cavendish (Malaysia) Sdn Bhd, Times Subang, Lot 46, Subang Hi-Tech Industrial Park, Batu Tiga, 40000 Shah Alam, Selangor Darul Ehsan, Malaysia

National Library Board, Singapore Cataloguing-in-Publication Data

Name(s): Tan, Phay Shing.
Title: Macaron basics : an illustrated step-by-step guide / Tan Phay Shing.
Description: Singapore : Marshall Cavendish Cuisine, [2018] | Series: Creative baking.
Identifier(s): OCN 1043049604 | ISBN 978-981-48-2860-4 (paperback)
Subject(s): LCSH: Macarons. | LCGFT: Cookbooks.
Classification: DDC 641.8654--dc23

Printed in Singapore

Contents

Introduction

It has been almost three years since I published my first book on macarons. Between then and now, I have experimented with more recipes, designs and techniques, and I can't wait to share them with you! While I received positive feedback about how helpful the first book, Creative Baking: Macarons, was, and how beautiful the designs were, I also had feedback that some could not get the hang of making Italian meringue.

This book has thus been written with this in mind — to help home bakers overcome the various challenges they may face in making macarons, while providing even greater detail on the various techniques.

To this end, I have included a basic recipe for making the meringue using the French method because it is easier and does not require the use of a candy thermometer nor a stand mixer. The French method is also more suitable for home bakers who may only want to make a small quantity of macarons.

Although this book features fewer designs than *Creative Baking: Macarons*, it more than makes up for it by including all the basic techniques you need to know in order to create interesting features, designs and even structures. With this, you can come up with any creative design of your own! The designs in this book have been carefully curated, such that they are not too complex, yet relevant for a host of celebratory occasions, from Valentine's Day to Christmas and Chinese New Year, so you may share these cute and delectable treats with your family and friends.

I have also included new recipes for fillings that are yummy and not too sweet, and which will hold up even in hot and humid Singapore, and simplified previous recipes so they can be whipped up without too much fuss.

I hope you'll master the art of making these cute macarons with this book and the video tutorials linked to the recipes. Don't give up if things don't turn out well the first time — my first attempt at making macarons looked more tuiles!

Happy Baking!

Phay Shing

1
2
3
4
TARE
ON
OFF
5
6
7
8
9
10
11
12

Basic Tools & Equipment

1 **Electric Mixer**

An electric mixer is useful for whipping up the meringue which forms the base of macarons. You can use either a handheld mixer or stand mixer for both French and Italian methods, but a stand mixer is preferable for making Italian meringue so you don't have to hold the mixer while adding the boiling syrup. If working with just a small volume of egg whites, a handheld mixer is preferable.

2 **Mixing Bowls**

Having several mixing bowls of different sizes on hand is useful when making macarons. Use a medium or large stainless steel mixing bowl for whisking meringue. Before using, wipe the bowl with a paper towel and some lemon juice or vinegar to remove any residual grease. The presence of grease may affect the foaming properties of the egg whites.

Use a heavy mixing bowl if using a handheld mixer. Use a medium bowl for mixing the mass (mixture of almond powder, icing sugar and egg white) in the Italian method, or holding the powdered ingredients in the French method. Smaller bowls will be useful for mixing batters of different colours.

3 **Sieve**

It is necessary to sift almond flour, icing sugar and other powdered ingredients such as cocoa powder and food colouring to break up any lumps and aerate the mixture. Large pieces of almond that are unable to pass through the fine mesh of the sieve should be discarded to ensure that the baked macaron shells have a smooth surface.

4 **Kitchen Scale**

Ingredients have to be weighed with precision for the macarons to turn out well consistently. Measuring the ingredients by volume using cups and spoons introduces more variation between batches of macarons. Choose a digital weighing scale that is able to measure at least 1 g as the smallest unit of measurement.

5 Candy Thermometer

When using the Italian meringue method of making macarons which uses hot sugar syrup, it is necessary to measure the temperature of the syrup before adding it to the egg whites. Hence, a candy thermometer or sugar thermometer is essential. The syrup needs to reach 115°C, also known as the soft ball stage, before it can be incorporated into the egg whites.

6 Oven Thermometer

It is helpful to have an oven thermometer in the oven throughout the baking time so you can monitor the temperature and ensure the macarons bake evenly. Macarons made using the Italian meringue method are typically baked at temperatures ranging from 130°C–140°C, and macarons made using the French method are typically baked at temperatures ranging from 140°C–150°C.

Light coloured shells are typically baked at a slightly lower temperature for a longer time to prevent the shells from browning while making sure that they are thoroughly cooked inside. An oven thermometer will allow you to have better control of the actual temperature of the oven for different coloured shells. Do bear in mind that individual ovens work differently, so learn to understand your oven and adjust the baking times and temperatures as necessary.

7 Baking Paper

I line the baking trays with baking paper when making macarons, so it is not necessary to use a silicone baking mat if you do not already own one. Choose heavy-duty baking paper that is non-stick and heat-resistant for the best results.

8 Baking Trays

Any type of metal baking tray that fits into your oven is suitable, although different metals conduct heat differently, so you may want to monitor your first batch of macarons more carefully.

Have several baking trays on hand as some recipes make 80–100 shells, depending on size, and the piped batter needs to be left on the trays to dry before baking.

The design templates provided in this book are meant to be enlarged by 200% on the photocopier, and printed on A4 size paper. Place the template on the baking tray under the sheet of baking paper. Baking trays that can fit an A4 sheet comfortably will do. For these recipes, I used trays measuring 35-cm x 25-cm.

9 Spatula

Choose a spatula with a firm wooden handle or a very stiff plastic handle to enable you to better handle the mass (mixture of almond powder, icing sugar and egg white) for the Italian method as it has a very thick consistency.

10 Piping Tips and Piping Bags

Round piping tips 4–7 mm in diameter are typically used for piping the base shells. Smaller piping tips 1–3 mm in diameter are used for piping features on the base shells. It is useful to have multiple piping tips of the same size on hand if working with various colours of batter.

I usually use small disposable plastic piping bags when piping fancy shapes for better control. Disposable bags also do away with the need for washing multiple bags if working with various colours of batter.

11 Toothpicks

In making creative macarons, toothpicks are used for nudging piped macaron batter into tight corners to create a more defined shape, or for pulling the batter to create fine features that stick out from the main shell body. Toothpicks are also used for nudging royal icing into tight corners or painting fine royal icing features onto baked shells.

12 Edible Ink Markers

Besides piping features on the baked shells using royal icing, edible ink markers can also be used for drawing fine features. As the ink may smudge when in contact with moisture, do not use markers to draw on royal icing for macarons that require refrigeration. The ink may also transfer and it is thus advisable not to stack the macarons if using ink markers.

1
2
5
3
4

Basic Ingredients

1

Almond Powder (Superfine)

This finely ground powder is a key ingredient in making macarons. Almond powder made from blanched almonds will ensure a more even colour for your macarons as the brown almond skin has been removed. Choose almond powder that has been very finely ground (superfine) so it is easier to sift. You may choose to grind your own almonds, but buying them already ground saves time. Almond powder can also be substituted with other ground nuts such as hazelnuts, cashews and pecans.

2

Icing Sugar

Also known as confectioner's sugar, this fine, powdered sugar is another main ingredient in making macarons. Some manufacturers mix cornstarch into the icing sugar to prevent clumping, and I have used both pure icing sugar or icing sugar with cornstarch to make macarons and found no significant difference in the quality of the macarons.

3

Sugar

Any type of granulated sugar can be used for making the syrup in the Italian method. For the French method, it is better to use fine white sugar, or castor sugar, as it will dissolve more easily in the egg whites during whisking.

4

Egg Whites

Fresh or aged egg whites are both suitable when making macarons, although the French method may benefit from using egg whites that have a lower water content through the ageing process. However, I find that separating the eggs in advance saves me time on the day I plan to bake. If you prefer to age your egg whites, place them in a bowl, cover with a paper towel and refrigerate for 1–2 days. Always let the egg whites come to room temperature before using.

5

Food Colouring

Use gel or powdered food colouring but not liquid food colouring in macaron batter to avoid introducing liquid into the batter. Liquid will hinder proper drying of the shells. I prefer to use natural food colouring although the colours tend to be subdued and may need to be enhanced using artificial colouring.

Macarons 101

Reducing sugar

Sugar gives macaron shells structure and shape. Reducing sugar in the recipe without replacement will compromise the structural stability of the shells. Choose savoury (e.g. salted caramel), sour (e.g. lemon) or bitter (e.g. dark chocolate or matcha) fillings to offset the sweetness of the shells. To reduce the amount of sugar, replace icing sugar with almond powder or rice flour and a pinch of cornflour. You may replace up to 15 per cent of the icing sugar without compromising the structure and texture.

Processing almond powder

If the almond powder you are using is not superfine, process it to make it easier to sift and ensure that the macarons have a smooth finish. Alternatively, sift more almond powder than what the recipe calls for to obtain the amount needed. Discard the larger bits that do not pass through the sieve.

Ageing egg whites

There has been a lot of discussion among bakers about the necessity of ageing egg whites for making macarons. Egg whites are aged to reduce the level of moisture in the batter, but this is not necessary.

Storing excess macaron batter

Macarons are best baked from freshly prepared batter, but should there be any batter left over, keep the batter in the piping bag and wrap the piping tip tightly with plastic wrap. Secure the top end of the piping bag with tape such that the batter is kept in an airtight condition. Store refrigerated for no more than a day. I have tried baking macarons with day-old batter and they turned out almost as usual.

Using the fan mode when baking

Although some people get beautiful macarons when using the fan mode of their ovens, others, like me, tend to end up with shells that are browned, lopsided and/or uneven on the surface. I suggest using the fan only towards the last 5 minutes of baking to dry out the shells thoroughly when the temperature is 110°C.

Resting piped batter before baking

Resting the piped batter allows a membrane to form on the surface. This will prevent the shells from cracking during baking and ensure the formation of the macaron "feet" which are the ruffles on the edges of the shell. If you are pressed for time, speed up the process by placing the piped batter in a 50–60°C-oven (fan mode off) for 5–10 minutes, then air-dry until the shells are dry to the touch.

Using cream of tartar to increase stability of meringue

I find it helps to add cream of tartar to the egg whites, when using the French method, as the egg whites are raw. I find it optional to add cream of tartar to the Italian meringue as the meringue is rather stable by nature given that the egg whites are partially cooked.

Using a handheld mixer when making Italian meringue

Before I got a stand mixer, I suspended the candy thermometer over the pot of boiling syrup with a pair of tongs while whisking the egg whites with a hand whisk until the soft peak stage. Once the syrup reached 115°C, I switched to a handheld mixer. Use a heavy metal bowl for whipping the meringue so it doesn't spin around as you pour the syrup with one hand and operate the handheld mixer with the other.

Cutting a hole in the piping bag instead of using a round piping tip

You may do this if you are piping very simple shapes and you are not particular about the macarons turning out slightly differently from shell to shell. Macarons with complex shapes require the use of precise tip sizes for the final product to turn out well.

Consuming macarons immediately after filling

Macarons taste better after being left to mature for 1–3 days. During this time, the shells will absorb moisture and flavour from the filling and soften slightly, so while they can be consumed immediately, waiting will allow them to taste better.

Baking two trays at a time

I would not recommend baking two trays at a time unless you are using a commercial oven as macarons are sensitive to the baking temperature. If using a home oven, the shells on the upper tray may brown too much if the temperature is higher at the top, and the shells on the lower tray may end up being hollow if the temperature is lower at the bottom. You may try to switch the position of the trays halfway through baking to see if it works, but it will be a risk as the temperature on each rack is hard to control for home ovens.

Designing a macaron template

You can search for soft copies of images that you like or do your own drawings on paper and scan them. Once you have your image, use an edge detection function of an imaging software to help you obtain a line drawing of the image. You can then copy the line drawing image into a Word document and resize it. Macarons typically measure 4–6 cm, so resize the image according to your preferred size. Copy and paste the image several times on the Word document for half the shells, and fill the other half of the document with a mirror image of the original line drawing if the image is not symmetrical. Keep each image at least 1 cm apart or have a wider margin between shells if you are new to baking macarons.

Using paper template during baking and risk of burning

Printing paper for home/office inkjet printers are able to withstand baking temperatures without burning. I have not had a single incident of the paper template burning in the oven.

Preparing several colours of batter for a batch of macarons

This is more specific to the Italian method as I do not recommend splitting a batch of French method batter into several colours. If using the French method, prepare separate batches of batter if working with more than 3 colours. If using the Italian method, prepare a batch of uncoloured mass and divide it into portions for the different colours. You may portion out the mass based on the estimated area that each colour covers for your subject. The weight of the Italian meringue should be half of the mass. You will end up with a little excess meringue which can be used to stick the baking paper onto the baking tray.

Making Macaron Batter Using the French Method

Makes 10–14 macarons

Scan the QR code to view a video tutorial on making macaron batter using the French method.

Ingredients

50 g almond powder

50 g icing sugar

A pinch of salt (optional)

Desired food colouring (powder or gel)

Meringue

40 g egg whites, at room temperature

$^{1}/_{8}$ tsp cream of tartar (optional)

36 g castor sugar

Tip

The yield of this recipe will vary with the size and shape of the macarons. As a rough guide, these quantities will produce batter sufficient for 20–28 shells or 10–14 macarons. Feel free to scale the recipe up to suit your needs. The French method is my preferred method when I need to make a small batch of macarons within a short time.

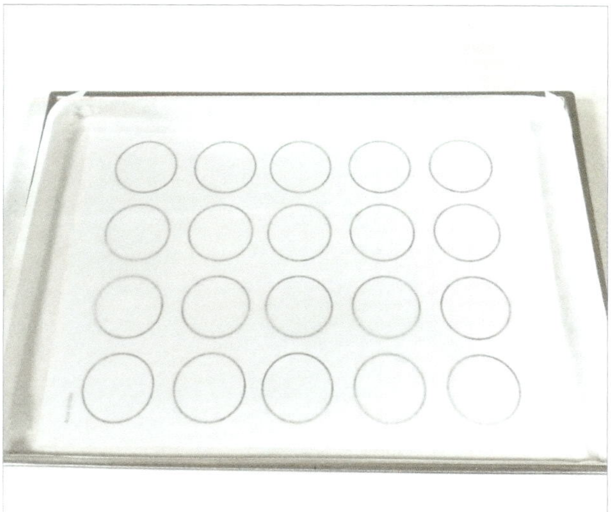

1. Place paper template on baking tray and line with baking paper. When meringue is ready, dab some on four corners of baking tray to keep baking paper from moving around.

2. Sift together almond powder, icing sugar and salt. If using powder food colouring, sift together as well. Set aside.

3. Prepare French meringue (see Note). In a clean, grease-free mixing bowl, beat egg whites with cream of tartar at medium speed until foamy. Gradually add castor sugar and beat until stiff peaks form. The meringue should appear smooth and glossy, and be able to hold a peak that can stand upright.

4. If using gel food colouring, add it to the meringue and use the electric mixer to beat for a few seconds or gently fold in the colouring using a spatula.

5. Prepare macaron batter. Sprinkle half the sifted dry ingredients over the meringue. Gently fold in until almost incorporated. Add the second half of the dry ingredients and gently fold in until totally incorporated.
6. You may adjust the colour of the batter at this point by adding more colouring if needed. Gently fold in the additional colouring.

7. At this point, the batter is under-mixed. You will need to deflate it to obtain the right consistency. Using a spatula, bring the batter from the base of the bowl up and press it against the side of the bowl while slowly turning the bowl. This is known as the press and fold technique.

8. Test to see if the consistency is right. Scoop a generous dollop of batter and watch how it falls back into the mixing bowl. An under-mixed batter will fall in a discontinuous manner whereas batter that is ready to be piped falls off the spatula in an almost continuous ribbon (as shown).

9. Alternatively, create small peaks in the batter, then tap the bottom of the bowl. The peaks should flatten out and disappear into the batter.
10. Repeat to fold and test until you achieve the right consistency.

NOTE You can also prepare the meringue using the Swiss method. Place the egg whites, cream of tartar and castor sugar in a mixing bowl set over a pot of simmering water. The water should not touch the bowl. Whisk by hand until the sugar is dissolved and the egg whites do not feel grainy. A candy thermometer should read 50°C. Remove from the heat and beat using an electric mixer until the meringue forms stiff peaks. The Swiss meringue is more stable than the meringue in the French method, making it a good option if you need to work with the macaron batter over a few hours.

Making Macaron Batter Using the Italian Method

Makes 40–50 macarons

Mass

200 g almond powder

200 g icing sugar

1/8 tsp salt (optional)

80 g egg whites, at room temperature

Desired food colouring (powder or gel)

Meringue

80 g egg whites, at room temperature

200 g castor sugar

75 g water

1/8 tsp cream of tartar (optional)

Tip

The yield of this recipe will vary with the size and shape of macarons. As a rough guide, these quantities will produce batter sufficient for 80–100 shells or 40–50 macarons. You may scale it up or down (up to half) according to your needs but I find that this portion is the most comfortable to work with. The Italian method is my preferred method when I need to make a large batch of macarons and/or if I have to work with multiple colours.

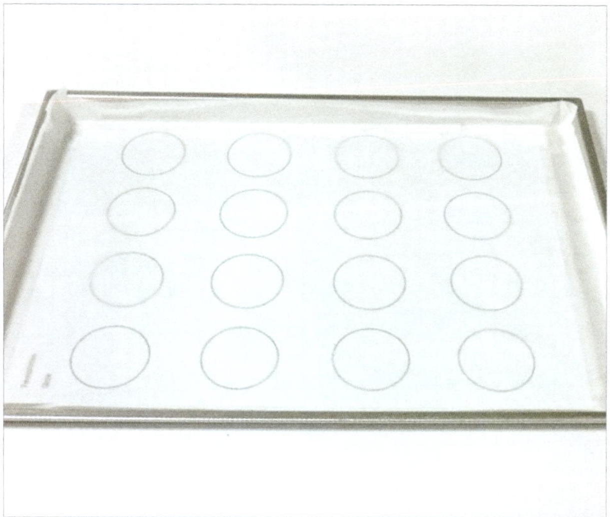

1. Place paper template on baking tray and line with baking paper. When meringue is ready, dab some on four corners of baking tray to keep baking paper from moving around.

2. Prepare mass. Sift together almond powder, icing sugar and salt, if using. Add egg whites and mix well.
3. Add a little food colouring and mix well. Bear in mind that the shade will lighten when meringue is folded in.

4. Prepare Italian meringue. In a clean, grease-free mixing bowl, beat egg whites at medium-low speed until foamy and opaque, and any peaks that form are soft and melt back into themselves after a second. This is known as the soft peak stage. Do not beat past this stage or the meringue will be too stiff to incorporate into the mass. Reduce mixer speed if necessary to keep egg whites moving.

5. While egg whites are beating, heat sugar and water in a small saucepan until mixture reaches 115–118°C on a candy thermometer. Stop stirring once sugar has dissolved to avoid crystals forming. Remove from heat immediately when temperature is reached.

6. Turn mixer speed to medium-high. Slowly and carefully pour hot syrup into egg whites, taking care to avoid whisk. When syrup has been incorporated, increase to high speed and beat for about 10 minutes or until meringue is cool. You should get stiff, glossy peaks when whisk is slowly lifted. Reserve a tablespoonful of meringue for sticking baking paper on baking tray.

7. Prepare macaron batter. Fold Italian meringue into mass. You do not have to be too gentle when folding as the meringue needs to be deflated slightly to obtain the right consistency.
8. Using a spatula and starting from the right, bring batter from bottom of bowl up to the other side.

9. Flip batter over, then press spatula downwards and towards side of bowl nearest you. Repeat steps, turning mixing bowl slowly as you fold. This is known as the press and fold technique.

10. When batter looks evenly mixed, test consistency. Scoop a dollop of batter and watch how it falls back into the bowl. An under-mixed batter will fall in a discontinuous manner. Continue folding and test again.
11. When batter falls off the spatula in a slow, magma-like way, forming a ribbon but breaking off at a few points, it is ready for piping fancy shaped macarons.
12. If piping round macarons, continue folding until batter is just able to fall off the spatula in an almost continuous ribbon, breaking off at a couple of points. Be careful not to overfold, or the batter will be too runny and the macarons won't turn out well.

Piping and Baking Macaron Shells

Scan the QR code to view a video tutorial on piping macaron batter.

1. Cut the tip off a disposable piping bag and fit your preferred piping tip into the hole. Use a round tip (4–7 mm) to pipe regular round shells and a small tip (1–3 mm) to pipe fine details.
2. Place the piping bag into a tall glass or mug, then fold the excess bag over the edges of the glass/mug.

3. Scoop macaron batter into bag.

   NOTE Although macaron batter is fairly stable, it is best to transfer it into the piping bag as soon as it is ready or keep it covered with plastic wrap touching the surface of the batter to prevent a crust forming.

4. Pipe shells on baking paper using paper template as a guide. Hold piping bag perpendicular to tray, with tip 5–7 mm away from baking paper.

   NOTE It is important to keep the tip in this perpendicular position and distance away from the baking paper in order to have nicely piped shells. You may rest your elbows on the table to steady your hands. Go slow if you are new to this. Practice makes perfect!

5. Press piping bag lightly to start piping. Release pressure on the piping bag when the batter is 2–3 mm away from the outline of the template as the batter will spread a little.
6. Give a little tip a little twirl before lifting tip off.
7. Hold baking paper down and hit tray hard on the worktop several times to release any trapped air bubbles. The peaks will flatten with tapping.

8. Leave shells to dry for 30 minutes to 2 hours, or until shells are dry to the touch and do not stick to your finger when you run it across the surface. In hot and humid climates, you may need to let the shells dry in an air-conditioned room or well-ventilated place with a fan.

   NOTE Baking when the piped batter is still sticky will result in cracked shells. Leaving the piped batter out to dry for too long will result in poor feet formation.

9. Set oven rack on the lowest or second lowest position and preheat the oven. If your oven temperature is uneven, rotate the tray halfway through baking.

   NOTE Use an oven thermometer to monitor the temperature of the oven at all times. This is important as home ovens can be off by 10°C to 20°C from the temperature set.

   The temperature and time for baking depends on the colour and size of the shells, and individual oven behaviour. Macarons made using the French method need higher starting temperatures than those made using the Italian method.

10. Bake macarons using the French method at 150°C for the first 10 minutes, then 130°C for 5–10 minutes or until the feet do not appear wet.
11. Bake macarons using the Italian method at 140°C for the first 10 minutes, then 130°C for 7–10 minutes or until the feet do not appear wet.
12. For pastel or white-coloured shells, reduce the oven temperature to 110°C after 8–10 minutes and continue baking for 7–15 minutes.

    NOTE Although I recommended a steady baking temperature for different coloured shells in my first book, I find that starting off at a higher temperature, then lowering it after the internal structure has set is better for preventing browning of shells, especially for lighter colours.

13. Remove from oven and let shells cool on tray before removing by gently peeling baking paper away. If feet appear a little wet, return tray to oven and bake at 110°C for another 5 minutes before checking again.
14. Do not attempt to remove shells from baking sheet if they are stuck as this means they are under baked.

15. If shells appear to be browning, check that oven temperature has not exceeded 110°C. Bake for a few minutes and check again.
16. Store cooled shells in an airtight container if not using immediately.

Storing and Filling Macaron Shells

1. Macaron shells can be prepared in advance and kept frozen for up to 3 months.
2. To freeze shells, place between layers of baking paper in an airtight container.
3. Thaw at room temperature without opening the container, then decorate and/or fill as desired.

4. Freezing shells without any filling may alter the texture of the shells and cause them to become less delicate, so you may want to brush the bottom of the shells with syrup or cream to soften the shells slightly before filling.

5. Prepare desired filling and spoon into a small piping bag. Cut a small hole at the tip. Pipe filling onto half the shells and sandwich with the other half.
6. If using two types of filling, pipe a ring of the first filling on the shell, then pipe the other filling in the centre.

Making Royal Icing

Royal Icing

250 g icing sugar

18 g meringue powder

$^1/_8$ tsp salt (optional)

43 g cool boiled water

A few drops of vanilla extract or other flavouring (optional)

Gel food colouring

Tip

After the macarons have been baked, it's time to start decorating! Royal icing can be prepared in a variety of colours to create fine details on macarons. A stiffer icing is used as glue for joining parts of a macaron structure.

a

1. Sift icing sugar, meringue powder and salt, if using, into a mixing bowl. Gradually add water and flavouring, if using, and beat with a hand whisk for 5–6 minutes, or with a handheld mixer for 3 minutes on low speed.
2. Adjust consistency if necessary by adding more water (flooding consistency for decorating) or icing sugar (stiff consistency for construction of macaron structures).
3. To test for flooding consistency (a), lift the whisk and allow icing to fall back into bowl. Any peaks in the icing should disappear in about 10 seconds.

b

4. Stiff icing (b) should be able to hold stiff peaks which are upright.
5. Colour icing as desired.

   NOTE Royal icing is typically off-white in colour. Use white gel food colouring to make it pure white. For black royal icing, use charcoal powder. For brown royal icing, use cocoa powder with brown gel food colouring.
6. Royal icing will keep refrigerated for up to 1 month. Store in an airtight container with plastic wrap touching the surface of icing. Stir well before use.

Making Macaron Fillings

Dark Chocolate Ganache

90 g dark chocolate, chopped
9 g unsalted butter
30 g heavy cream
$^{1}/_{8}$ tsp fine sea salt
$^{1}/_{2}$ tsp vanilla bean paste

1. Place all ingredients in a microwave-safe bowl and heat in a microwave oven for 20 seconds at medium power. Mix well with a spatula. Repeat heating and mixing until chocolate is melted and ganache is smooth.
2. Let sit at room temperature for about 30 minutes to firm up to consistency of toothpaste before using.
3. For a lighter texture, chill ganache in the freezer for 2 minutes, then mix with a spatula. Repeat chilling and mixing until ganache firms up, then whip to texture of buttercream.

   NOTE This is a fairly firm ganache and is suitable for using in warmer climates. Increase the quantity of heavy cream to 40-45 g if you stay in a cooler climate or prefer a softer ganache.

Lemon Curd

45 g unsalted butter, at room temperature
112 g castor sugar
1 large egg (65 g)
1 large egg yolk
80 g freshly squeezed lemon juice
$^{1}/_{2}$ tsp finely grated lemon zest

1. Using an electric mixer, beat butter and sugar at medium speed for about 2 minutes until creamy. Gradually add egg and egg yolk and beat for 1 minute. Mix in lemon juice. The mixture will appear to curdle, but this is fine.
2. Cook mixture over low heat, stirring constantly until smooth. Increase heat to medium and keep stirring until mixture thickens and coats the back of a wooden spoon. Do not let mixture boil. Remove from heat and stir in lemon zest.
3. Transfer to a bowl and press plastic wrap on surface of curd to keep a skin from forming. Chill before use. Lemon curd will keep for up to a week refrigerated and up to 2 months in the freezer.

Salted Caramel

100 g castor sugar

2 Tbsp water

60 g heavy cream

15 g unsalted butter

1 tsp fine sea salt

1 tsp vanilla extract

1. Place sugar and water in a deep, light coloured saucepan. This is so the colour of the syrup will be visible. Cook over medium heat without stirring until golden brown in colour. Watch the solution carefully to avoid burning. You may gently swirl the solution in the saucepan for it to cook more evenly.
2. Turn off heat and carefully add cream while stirring using a long wooden spoon. Be careful as the mixture will bubble up. Keep stirring until the mixture settles.
3. Add butter, salt and vanilla extract and mix well.
4. Set aside to cool before using or storing in an airtight container. Salted caramel will keep for up to a week refrigerated or up to 3 months in the freezer.

Berry Jams

100 g fresh berries (if using strawberries, chop into smaller pieces)

15–25 g castor sugar

A pinch of salt

1 tsp lemon juice

$^{1}/_{2}$ tsp cornstarch dissolved in a bit of water (optional)

1. Place berries, sugar, salt and lemon juice in a small saucepan and bring to a boil. Lower heat to a simmer and stir continuously for 15–20 minutes until mixture is thickened.
2. If jam is still too watery for your liking, add cornstarch slurry to thicken further.
3. Set aside to cool completely before straining to remove seeds. Refrigerate until ready to use. Berry jams can be made in advance and stored in airtight containers.

NOTE Raspberries, strawberries, blueberries and blackberries make excellent macaron fillings as their tartness offsets the sweetness of macaron shells well. Adjust the amount of sugar added according to your taste preference or the tartness of the berries.

The part of the shell in contact with the jam will soften over time, so macarons with jam filling should be consumed within a week of assembly.

Vanilla Swiss Meringue Buttercream (SMBC)

75 g egg whites (from 2 large eggs)

A pinch of salt

50 g castor sugar

135 g unsalted butter, at room temperature, cut into cubes

1 tsp vanilla extract

1. Prepare a deep saucepan and a heatproof bowl that will sit snugly in the mouth of the pan. Fill pan with water to a depth of 2.5 cm and place over low heat. Place egg whites, salt and sugar in heatproof bowl and place into pan.
2. Using a hand whisk or handheld mixer, whisk egg whites at medium-low speed for 5–6 minutes until sugar has melted and mixture is foamy. The temperature should read 71.1°C on a candy thermometer.
3. Remove bowl from heat and continue beating at high speed for about 10 minutes until mixture is stiff and glossy, and has cooled to 30°C. Scrape down sides of bowl from time to time to ensure mixture is even.
4. Add a cube of butter and beat at medium speed until butter is incorporated. Do not worry if the mixture appears to curdle. Continue adding and incorporating butter a cube at a time. When all the butter has been added, increase speed and beat for 1–2 minutes until the mixture is light and fluffy. Add vanilla and beat well until incorporated. Use as desired.
5. SMBC can be prepared up to a month in advance. Place in a resealable plastic bag and store in the freezer. Bring to room temperature and whisk until light and fluffy before using.
6. To make berry-flavoured or lemon SMBC, add 75–85 g berry jam or lemon curd to 250 g basic SMBC and mix well. To make salted caramel SMBC, add 100 g salted caramel to 200 g basic SMBC.

NOTE Swiss meringue buttercream is often used as a base for different flavours of macaron filling because it is light and versatile. Here is a basic recipe for a low sugar version which goes perfectly with the sweet shells. This recipe makes about 250 g SMBC. Jazz it up with your favourite ingredients. I have provided some suggestions to vary the basic buttercream in point 6 above. The quantities can be adjusted according to taste.

Tea-flavoured White Chocolate Ganache

110 g white chocolate, chopped
20 g unsalted butter
30 g heavy cream
1/4 tsp vanilla bean paste
1/4 tsp fine sea salt
1–1 1/2 tsp tea powder, sifted

1. Place all ingredients except tea powder in a microwave-safe bowl and heat in the microwave oven for 20 seconds at medium-low power. Mix well with a spatula. Repeat heating and mixing until chocolate is melted and mixture is smooth. Be careful not to over-heat white chocolate or it will separate.
2. Add tea powder and mix well. Let sit at room temperature for about 30 minutes to firm up to consistency of toothpaste before using.
3. For a lighter texture, chill ganache in the freezer for 2 minutes, then mix with a spatula. Repeat chilling and mixing until ganache firms up before whipping to texture of buttercream.

NOTE Teas such as matcha, Earl Grey, osmanthus, lavender and rose are aromatic, and offset the sweetness of macaron shells well. You may use store-bought tea powder or make your own by drying the flowers/leaves in a 90°C-oven for 30 minutes, then grinding into powder. The flowers/leaves can also be infused in the heavy cream for a lighter flavour. The tea powder can be substituted with freeze-dried fruit powder. Adjust the quantity of fruit powder added according to taste.

Fruit-based White Chocolate Buttercream

110 g white chocolate, chopped
20 g unsalted butter
1/8 tsp fine sea salt
50–55 g berry jam (page 32) or fruit purée
1/4–1/2 tsp fruit flavouring (according to the type of berry jam or fruit purée used, optional)

1. Place white chocolate and butter in a microwave-safe bowl and heat in the microwave oven for 20 seconds at medium power. Mix well with a spatula. Repeat heating and mixing until mixture is smooth. Add salt and mix well.
2. Freeze bowl for 2 minutes and mix well with a spatula. Repeat freezing and mixing. As the mixture thickens, start to beat it with the spatula. You will notice that the texture will lighten and become creamy.
3. Add a teaspoon of berry jam or fruit purée (and fruit flavouring, if using) and whip mixture with the spatula until well combined. Repeat until all the berry jam or fruit purée has been added. The texture should be like buttercream.

NOTE This filling is adapted from the recipe for tea-flavoured white chocolate ganache. The heavy cream is replaced with berry jam or fruit purée. I experimented and found that this recipe allows you to have the highest fruit content without the filling being too soft, even in hot climates. Use home-made fruit jams if possible to get the most intense natural fruit flavour. Excellent flavours would be mango and all kinds of berries.

Basic Vanilla White Chocolate

100 g white chocolate, chopped

25 g vegetable shortening

1/4 tsp fine sea salt

1 tsp vanilla bean paste or extract

1 tsp lemon juice (to counter the sweetness of white chocolate, optional)

1. Place white chocolate and vegetable shortening in a microwave-safe bowl and heat in the microwave oven for 10–20 seconds at medium-low power. Stir to mix well. Repeat heating and mixing until melted and smooth. Alternatively, melt white chocolate and vegetable shortening over a pot of simmering water.
2. Add salt and mix well. Add vanilla gradually and mix well. Add lemon juice gradually and mix well. Do not add liquids all at once or chocolate mixture may seize.
3. Let sit at room temperature to firm up to consistency of toothpaste before using.

NOTE When you need a filling that holds up well in hot weather or for use in macaron structures where the filling has to remain firm, some options include peanut butter, dark chocolate and white chocolate-based fillings like this one. I use white chocolate as the base for making different flavours of fillings that do not require refrigeration, and these are usually citrus fruit-based (lemon or orange), sour fruit-based (passionfruit or berries) or tea-flavoured. For citrus flavours, add 1–1 1/2 tsp lemon/orange paste and 1/2 tsp finely grated zest. For sour fruit flavours, add 2–4 tsp freeze-dried fruit powder or fruit pastes. For tea flavours, add 2–4 tsp tea powder. Powders and pastes can be added according to taste.

Piping Circles

Big and Small Round Macarons

Italian Meringue Method

Makes three 13-cm macarons, four 6-cm macarons, twelve 3.5-cm macarons and twelve 2.5-cm macarons

Scan the QR code to view a video tutorial on piping large circles.

Mass

220 g almond powder

220 g icing sugar

1/4 tsp white powder food colouring (optional, to keep shells pastel)

88 g egg whites, at room temperature

Pink and red gel food colouring

1/8 tsp salt (optional)

Italian Meringue

88 g egg whites, at room temperature

220 g castor sugar

82 g water

1/8 tsp cream of tartar (optional)

Suggested Filling

Strawberry white chocolate (page 35)

Strawberry white chocolate buttercream (page 34), made using 50–55 g strawberry jam (page 32)

1. Prepare baking trays and circle template (pages 88–90 for different sizes of circles).
2. Prepare mass. Sift together almond powder, icing sugar, salt and white powder food colouring, if using. Add egg whites and mix well. Divide mass into 2 equal portions.
3. Add a little gel food colouring to each portion to get 2 shades of pink and mix well. Bear in mind that the shades will lighten when the meringue is folded in.

4. Prepare Italian meringue (page 20). Divide into 2 equal portions.
5. Prepare macaron batters (page 21). Fold meringue into masses.
6. Transfer each batter into a piping bag fitted with 6–7-mm round tip.

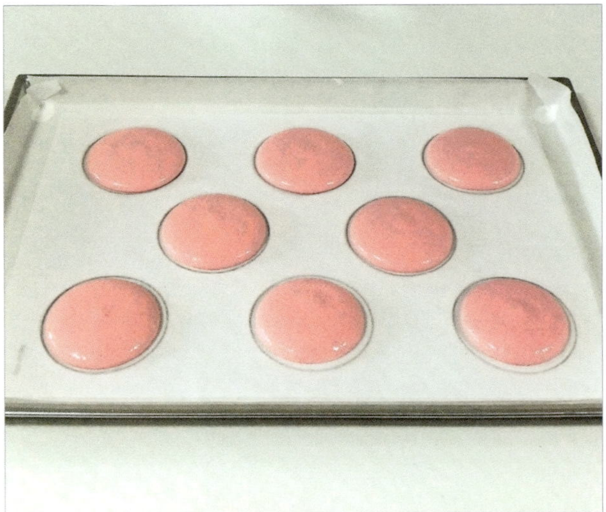

7. There are different ways of piping circles of different sizes.
8. For circles smaller than 7 cm in diameter, begin by positioning the piping tip above the centre of the circle template. Apply pressure on the piping bag to start piping, then release pressure on the piping bag when the batter is 2–3-mm away from the outline of the template. The batter will spread a little. Hit tray on worktop to release any trapped air bubbles.

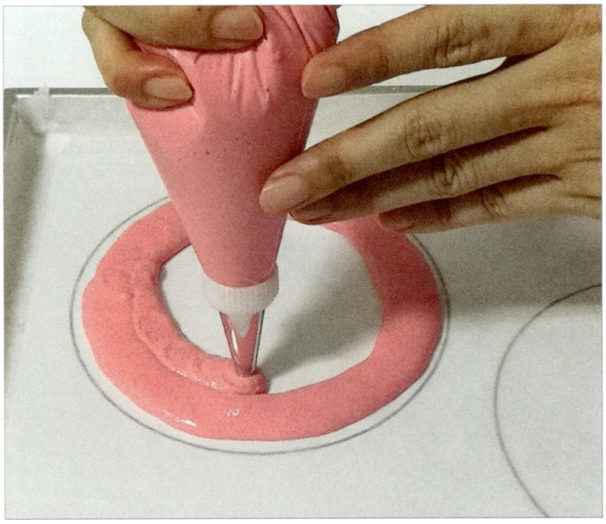

9. For circles larger than 8 cm in diameter, use the trace-and-fill technique (page 50) to pipe the circle. Begin by tracing the outline of the circle, leaving a 3–5-mm spacing between the batter and the outline of the circle.
10. Fill the circle with batter by piping concentric circles. Hit tray on worktop to release any trapped air bubbles.

11. Use a toothpick to nudge the batter where it is a little out of shape. Hit the tray again if needed.

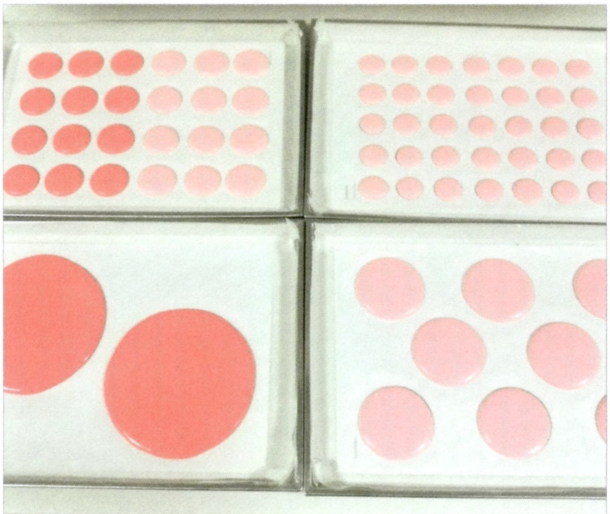

12. Let shells dry (page 24).
13. Bake in a preheated oven until feet do not appear wet:

    13-cm circle: 140°C for 15 minutes, then 130°C for 10 minutes and 20–25 minutes at 110°C;

    6-cm circle: 140°C for 10 minutes, then 130°C for 5 minutes and 110°C for 10–12 minutes;

    3.5 and 2.5 cm circles: 140°C for 10 minutes, then 110°C for about 8 minutes.

    NOTE When baking a batch of macarons with various sizes, pipes shells of similar sizes on the same tray as baking temperature and times vary for different sizes of shells.

14. Prepare and pipe filling.
15. For larger shells, you may wish to start with small dollops of a firmer filling like strawberry white chocolate around the circumference of the shell.

16. Then continue by piping concentric circles of strawberry white chocolate buttercream to fill the ring to create a simple but visually aesthetic look.
17. Store in an airtight container and refrigerate for at least 24 hours before serving.

Piping Hearts

Pastel Heart Macarons

Italian Meringue Method

Makes 40–50 macarons

Scan the QR code to view a video tutorial on piping heart shapes.

Mass

200 g almond powder

200 g icing sugar

$^1/_8$ tsp salt (optional)

$^1/_2$ tsp white powder food colouring (optional, to keep shells pastel)

80 g egg whites, at room temperature

Pink, yellow, green and blue gel food colouring

Italian Meringue

80 g egg whites, at room temperature

200 g castor sugar

75 g water

$^1/_8$ tsp cream of tartar (optional)

Suggested Filling

Mango white chocolate buttercream (page 34), made using 50–55 g mango purée

1. Prepare baking tray and heart template (page 90).
2. Prepare mass. Sift together almond powder, icing sugar, salt and white powder food colouring, if using. Add egg whites and mix well. Divide mass into 4 equal portions.
3. Add a little gel food colouring to each portion and mix well. Bear in mind that the shades will lighten when the meringue is folded in.

4. Prepare Italian meringue (page 20). Divide into 4 equal portions.
5. Prepare macaron batters (page 21). Fold meringue into masses.
6. Transfer each batter into a piping bag fitted with a 6-mm round tip.

7. To pipe a heart shape, start by piping a circle on the top left side of the heart, allowing the batter to spread until it is 2–3 mm away from the edge of the heart outline.

8. Then, move the piping tip to trace the "V" of the heart, constantly making sure that the batter spreads until it is 2–3 mm away from the edge of the heart outline.

9. End off by releasing pressure on the piping bag and swiping the piping tip down towards the pointed tip of the heart.

10. Use a toothpick to nudge the batter where necessary.
11. Hit tray on worktop to release any trapped air bubbles.

12. Let shells dry (page 24).
13. Bake in a preheated oven at 140°C for 10 minutes, then 110°C for 7–15 minutes or until feet do not appear wet.

14. Prepare and pipe filling.
15. Store in an airtight container and refrigerate for at least 24 hours before serving.

Piping Squares

Mortarboard Macarons

French Meringue Method

Makes 12–14 macarons

45 g almond powder

47 g icing sugar

6 g cocoa powder

4 g (2 tsp) charcoal powder

A pinch of salt (optional)

French Meringue

40 g egg whites, at room temperature

36 g castor sugar

$^{1}/_{8}$ tsp cream of tartar (optional)

A few drops of black gel food colouring (optional)

Finishing

Flooding consistency black royal icing (page 28)

Red sour candy strips, cut into 4 x 0.5-cm lengths, then make a slit at one end

Suggested Filling

Dark chocolate ganache (page 31)

Scan the QR code to view a video tutorial on piping squares.

1. Prepare baking tray and mortarboard template (page 91).
2. Sift together almond powder, icing sugar, cocoa powder, charcoal powder and salt. Set aside.
3. Prepare French meringue and macaron batter (page 16).
4. Transfer batter to a piping bag fitted with a 4-mm round tip.
5. Pipe circles (page 36).
6. Pipe squares by tracing outline of square, keeping batter 2–3-mm away from outline.

7. Fill middle with batter.
8. Use a toothpick to nudge batter where necessary.
9. Hit tray on worktop to release any trapped air bubbles.
10. Let shells dry (page 24).
11. Preheat oven to 150°C. Place tray on bottom or second lowest rack in oven, and bake for 10 minutes, then reduce oven temperature to 130°C and bake for 5–10 minutes or until feet do not appear wet.
12. Rotate tray halfway through baking. Let shells cool on tray before removing.

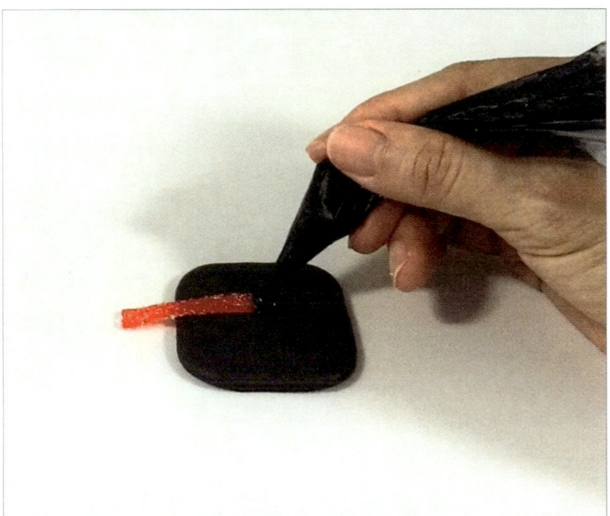

13. Make little snips at one end of sour candy strips to create tassel.
14. Prepare black royal icing. Spoon into a piping bag and cut a small hole at the tip.
15. Pipe a little icing in the middle of a square macaron shell. Stick a sour candy strip on the square, then pipe a circle of icing over to cover the end of the tassel. Set aside for an hour until icing is dry.
16. Prepare and pipe filling.
17. Store in an airtight container and refrigerate for at least 24 hours before serving.

Piping Triangles

Snow-capped Mountain Macarons

French Meringue Method

Makes 12–14 macarons

50 g almond powder

50 g icing sugar

1/2 tsp charcoal powder

A pinch of salt (optional)

French Meringue

40 g egg whites, at room temperature

36 g castor sugar

1/8 tsp cream of tartar (optional)

Finishing

Flooding consistency white royal icing (page 28)

Suggested Filling

Matcha white chocolate ganache (page 34)

Scan the QR code to view a video tutorial on piping triangles.

1. Prepare baking tray and mountain template (page 91).
2. Sift together almond powder, icing sugar, charcoal powder and salt. Set aside.
3. Prepare French meringue and macaron batter (page 16).
4. Transfer batter to a piping bag fitted with a 4-mm round tip.
5. Pipe triangles by tracing outline of triangle, keeping batter 2–3-mm away from outline.

6. Fill middle with batter.
7. Use a toothpick to nudge batter where necessary.
8. Hit tray on worktop to release any trapped air bubbles.
9. Let shells dry (page 24).
10. Preheat oven to 150°C. Place tray on bottom or second lowest rack in oven, and bake for 10 minutes, then reduce oven temperature to 130°C and bake for 5–10 minutes or until feet do not appear wet.

11. Rotate tray halfway through baking. Let shells cool on tray before removing.
12. Prepare white royal icing. Spoon royal icing into a piping bag and cut a small hole at the tip. Pipe some icing as snow at the peak of the mountain. Set aside for an hour until icing is dry.
13. Prepare and pipe filling.
14. Store in an airtight container and refrigerate for at least 24 hours before serving.

Creating Fine Features

Baby Chick Macarons

French Meringue Method

Makes 12–14 macarons

50 g almond powder

50 g icing sugar

A pinch of salt (optional)

French Meringue

40 g egg whites, at room temperature

36 g castor sugar

$^{1}/_{8}$ tsp cream of tartar (optional)

Yellow gel food colouring

Finishing

Black and orange edible food markers, or black and orange royal icing

Peach-coloured lustre dust

Suggested Filling

Salted caramel SMBC (page 33)

Salted caramel (page 32)

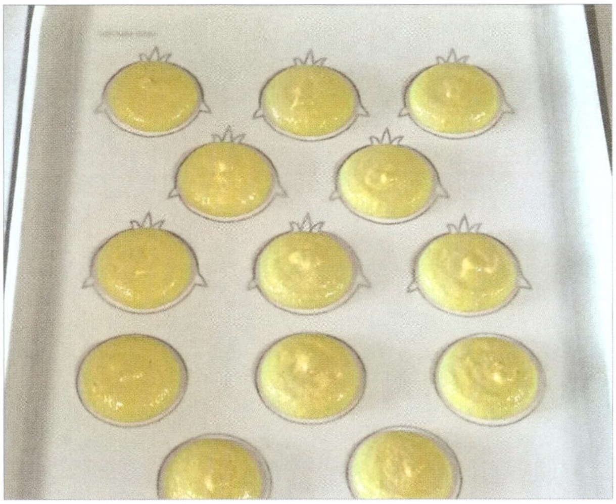

1. Prepare baking tray and chick template (page 92).
2. Sift together almond powder, icing sugar and salt. Set aside.
3. Prepare French meringue (page 16). Add a little yellow gel food colouring and gently fold in using a spatula or beat for a few seconds using the electric mixer.
4. Prepare macaron batter (page 16).
5. Transfer batter to a piping bag fitted with a 6–7-mm round tip. Pipe a circle for body of chick, keeping batter 2–3-mm away from outline.
6. Hit tray on worktop to release any trapped air bubbles.

7. Use a toothpick to pull the batter for hair and wings of chick for top shells.
8. Let shells dry (page 24).
9. Preheat oven to 150°C. Place tray on bottom or second lowest rack in oven, and bake for 10 minutes, then reduce oven temperature to 130°C and bake for 5–10 minutes or until feet do not appear wet.
10. Rotate tray halfway through baking. Let shells cool on tray before removing.

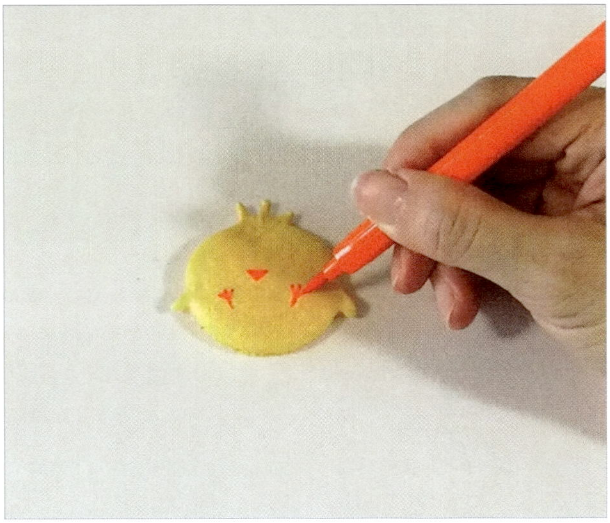

11. Draw beak and feet of chicks using orange edible food marker and eyes using black edible food marker.
12. Using a small dry brush, dab a little lustre dust for the cheeks.
13. Prepare and pipe filling.
14. Store in an airtight container and refrigerate for at least 24 hours before serving.

Creating Complex Shapes

Trace-and-Fill Technique

Unicorn Macarons

Italian Meringue Method

Makes 55–70 macarons

Scan the QR code to view a video tutorial on piping unicorns.

Mass

200 g almond powder

200 g icing sugar

1/8 tsp salt (optional)

1/4 tsp white powder food colouring (optional, to keep shells pastel)

80 g egg whites, at room temperature

White, blue and purple gel food colouring

Italian Meringue

80 g egg whites, at room temperature

200 g castor sugar

75 g water

1/8 tsp cream of tartar (optional)

Finishing

Black edible food marker

Suggested Filling

Strawberry white chocolate (page 35) or Strawberry white chocolate buttercream (page 34)

1. Prepare baking tray and unicorn template (page 92).
2. Prepare mass. Sift together almond powder, icing sugar, salt and white powder food colouring, if using. Add egg whites and mix well.
3. Divide mass into 3 portions in the ratio 6 (white) : 1 (blue) : 1 (purple). Add a little of the respective gel food colouring to each portion and mix well. Bear in mind that the shade will lighten when the meringue is folded in.

4. Prepare Italian meringue (page 20). Portion the meringue for each mass; each portion should be half the weight of the respective mass.
5. Prepare macaron batter (page 21). Fold meringue into mass.
6. Transfer white batter into a piping bag fitted with a 4-mm round tip. Transfer purple and blue batters into piping bags fitted with 2-3-mm round tips.

7. Pipe unicorn body using white batter by tracing outline, then filling spaces in the centre.

8. Use a toothpick to pull the batter for the ears and nudge the batter into corners to fill the shape.
9. Hit tray on worktop to release any trapped air bubbles.
10. Set aside for 15 minutes or until a thin membrane is formed.

11. Pipe horn using purple batter.
12. Pipe first, third and fifth segments of wings using purple batter. Set aside for 15 minutes or until a thin membrane forms. This will help create definition in the wings (page 59).

13. Pipe mane and tail with blue batter.

14. Pipe second and fourth segments of wings with purple batter.

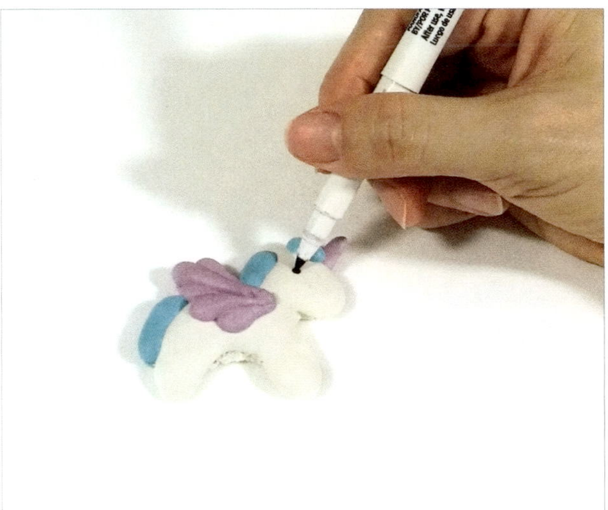

15. Let shells dry (page 24).
16. Preheat oven to 140°C. Place tray on bottom or second lowest rack in oven, and bake for 10 minutes, then reduce oven temperature to 110°C and bake for 7–10 minutes or until feet do not appear wet.
17. Rotate tray halfway through baking. Let shells cool on tray before removing.
18. Draw eyes of unicorn using black edible food marker.
19. Prepare and pipe filling.
20. Store in an airtight container and refrigerate for at least 24 hours before serving.

Creating Pop-up Features

Rose Macarons

Italian Meringue Method

Makes 30–40 macarons

Mass

200 g almond powder

200 g icing sugar

1/8 tsp salt (optional)

5 g freeze-dried raspberry powder (optional)

80 g egg whites, at room temperature

Pink and red gel food colouring

Italian Meringue

80 g egg whites, at room temperature

200 g castor sugar

75 g water

1/8 tsp cream of tartar (optional)

Suggested Filling

Raspberry white chocolate buttercream (page 34), made using 50–55 g raspberry jam (page 32)

1. Prepare baking tray and rose template (page 93).
2. Prepare mass. Sift together almond powder, icing sugar, salt and freeze-dried raspberry powder, if using. Add egg whites and mix well. Divide mass into 3 equal portions.
3. Add a little gel food colouring to each portion to get 3 shades of pink and mix well. Bear in mind that the shades will lighten when the meringue is folded in.

   NOTE You may divide the mass into as many portions as you want to create roses of different shades of pink and red, or leave it as a single colour.

4. Prepare Italian meringue (page 20). Divide meringue into 3 equal portions.
5. Prepare macaron batters (page 21). Fold meringue into masses.
6. Transfer each batter into a piping bag fitted with a 6-mm round tip.

7. Pipe rose by tracing the outline, then filling the spaces in the centre.
8. Hit tray on worktop to release any trapped air bubbles.

9. Set aside for 15 minutes or until a thin membrane is formed. At this point, the piped shell should feel a little sticky, but the batter should not stick to your finger when you touch it gently.

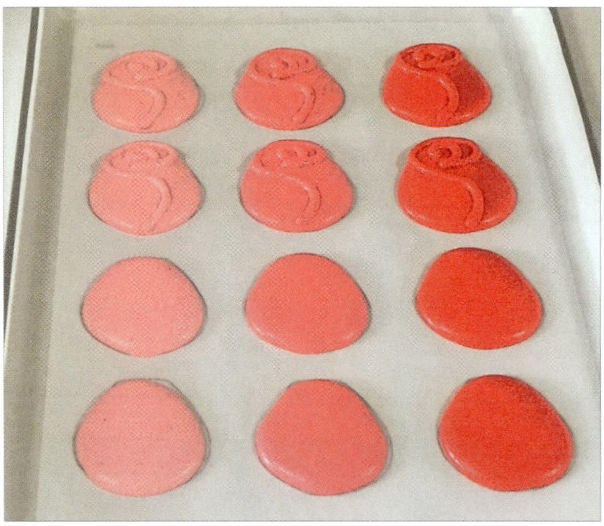

10. Change to a 2-mm round tip and pipe the definition of the rose petals. Do this for the top shells only.
11. Let shells dry (page 24).

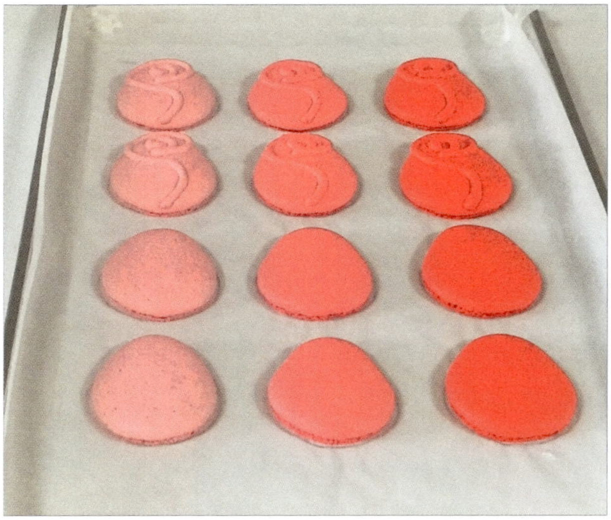

12. Preheat oven to 140°C. Place tray on bottom or second lowest rack in oven, and bake for 10 minutes, then reduce oven temperature to 110°C and bake for 7–15 minutes or until feet do not appear wet.
13. Rotate tray halfway through baking. Let shells cool on tray before removing.

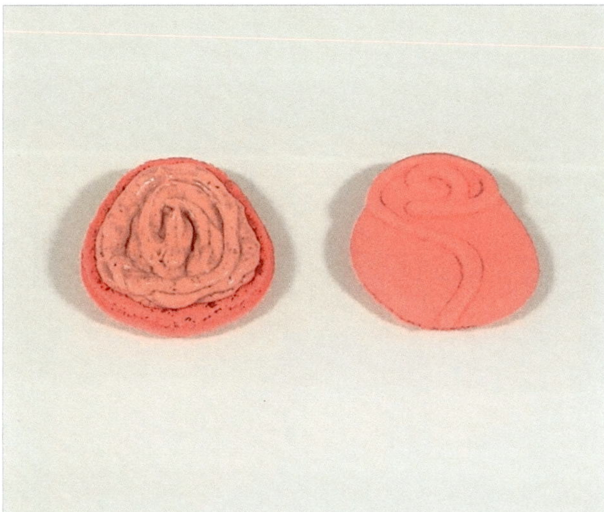

14. Prepare and pipe filling.

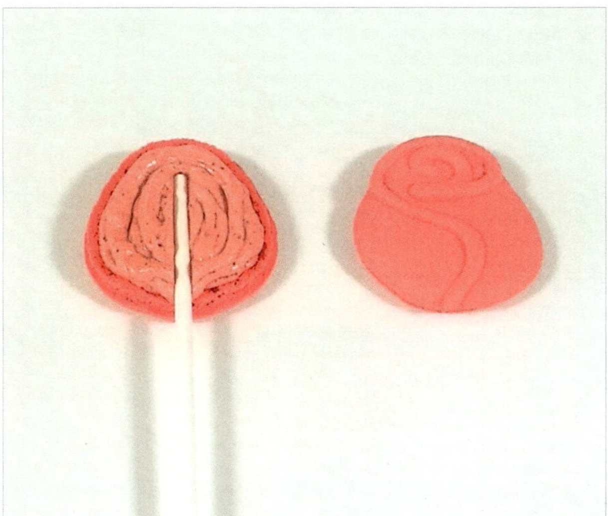

15. To arrange the roses on sticks, pipe the filling, then place a cakepop stick in the middle before covering with the other shell.
16. Store in an airtight container and refrigerate for at least 24 hours before serving.

Creating Definition

Scalloped Circle Macarons

Italian Meringue Method

Makes 5–7 large macarons

Mass

100 g almond powder

100 g icing sugar

A pinch of salt (optional)

$^{1}/_{8}$ tsp white powder food colouring (optional, to keep shells pastel)

40 g egg whites, at room temperature

Pink gel food colouring

Italian Meringue

40 g egg whites, at room temperature

100 g castor sugar

37 g water

A pinch of cream of tartar (optional)

Suggested Filling

Strawberry white chocolate (page 35)

Strawberry white chocolate buttercream (page 34), made using 50–55 g strawberry jam (page 32)

1. Prepare baking tray and scalloped circle template (page 93).
2. Prepare mass. Sift together almond powder, icing sugar, salt and white powder food colouring, if using. Add egg whites and mix well. Add a few drops of pink gel food colouring to the mass and mix well.
3. Prepare Italian meringue (page 20).
4. Prepare macaron batter (page 21). Fold the meringue into mass.

5. Transfer batter to a piping bag fitted with a 6-mm round tip.
6. Pipe alternate segments of the circle, starting from the outer edge inwards. Gradually release pressure on the piping bag as you pipe towards the centre of the circle.

7. Hit tray on worktop to release any trapped air bubbles.
8. Set aside for 15 minutes or until a thin membrane is formed.

9. Pipe in remaining segments, starting from the outer edge inwards. Gradually release pressure on the piping bag as you pipe towards the centre of the circle.

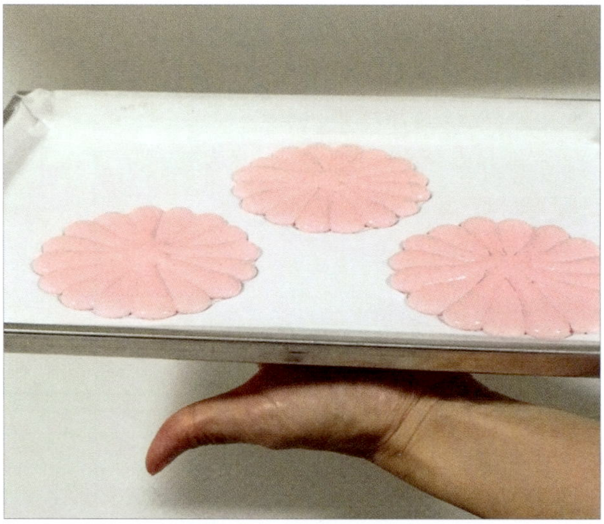

10. Gently tap the bottom of the tray to release any trapped air bubbles, being careful not to disturb the segments that were piped earlier.

11. Let shells dry (page 24).
12. Preheat oven to 140°C. Place tray on bottom or second lowest rack in oven, and bake for 10 minutes, then reduce oven temperature to 110°C and bake for 20–25 minutes or until feet do not appear wet.
13. Rotate tray halfway through baking. Let shells cool on tray before removing.

14. Prepare filling. Pipe a ring of strawberry white chocolate on the bottom shells.

15. Fill the middle with strawberry white chocolate buttercream.
16. Sandwich with the top shells.
17. Store in an airtight container and refrigerate for at least 24 hours before serving. If using this for the carousel roof, it may be assembled as soon as the outer ring of white chocolate is set.

Creating Indented Features

Happy Hippo Macarons

French Meringue Method

Makes 12–14 macarons

50 g almond powder

50 g icing sugar

A pinch of salt (optional)

French Meringue

40 g egg whites, at room temperature

36 g castor sugar

1/8 tsp cream of tartar (optional)

Purple/violet gel food colouring

Finishing

Black edible food marker

Suggested Filling

Blue or blackberry white chocolate buttercream (page 34), made using 50–55 g berry jam (page 32)

1. Prepare baking tray and hippo template (page 94).
2. Sift together almond powder, icing sugar and salt. Set aside.
3. Prepare French meringue (page 16). Add a little purple/violet gel food colouring and gently fold in using a spatula or beat for a few seconds using the electric mixer.

4. Prepare macaron batter (page 16).
5. Transfer batter to a piping bag fitted with a 4-mm round tip.

6. Pipe muzzle on top shell by piping an oval shape. Do not pipe the rest of the head for the top shell at this point.

7. Pipe bottom shell by tracing the outline, then filling the spaces in the centre.
8. Hit tray on worktop to release any trapped air bubbles.

9. Set aside for 15 minutes or until a thin membrane is formed. At this point, the piped shell should feel a little sticky, but the batter should not stick to your finger when you touch it gently.
10. Continue to pipe the rest of the head for the top shells.

11. Switch to a 2-mm round tip and pipe the ears for the top shells.
12. Gently tap the bottom of the tray to release any trapped air bubbles, being careful not to disturb the segments that were piped earlier.

13. Make indents for the nostrils using the blunt end of a toothpick.

    NOTE If the batter flows back to fill the indent, wait for another 5–10 minutes and try again. However, do not wait until a firm membrane forms or the membrane may crack.

14. Let shells dry (page 24).

15. Preheat oven to 150°C. Place tray on bottom or second lowest rack in oven, and bake for 10 minutes, then reduce oven temperature to 110°C and bake for 5–10 minutes or until feet do not appear wet.

    NOTE A lower oven temperature is used for the second of the baking time as purple-coloured shells tend to brown more easily.

16. Rotate tray halfway through baking. Let shells cool on tray before removing.
17. Draw eyes and mouth of hippo using black edible food marker.
18. Prepare and pipe filling.
19. Store in an airtight container and refrigerate for at least 24 hours before serving.

Creating Raised Smooth Features

Rosette Macarons

French Meringue Method

Makes 6 macarons

40 g almond powder

40 g icing sugar

1 tsp (2 g) cornflour, to thicken the batter

A pinch of salt

French Meringue

30 g icing sugar

20 g castor sugar

36 g egg whites, at room temperature

A pinch of cream of tartar (optional)

Yellow gel food colouring

Suggested Filling

Lemon SMBC (page 33)

Lemon curd (page 31)

1. Prepare baking tray and 5-cm circle template (page 94).
2. Sift together almond powder, icing sugar, cornflour and salt. Set aside.
3. Prepare French meringue (page 16). Mix together icing sugar and castor sugar in a small bowl before adding to egg whites.

4. Prepare macaron batter (page 16).

   NOTE When the powdered ingredients are just incorporated, use the spatula to press the batter to the side of the mixing bowl as you normally would for regular macarons to knock out some air. This is where a little trial and error is required. Overfolding may cause the batter to become too runny to hold sharp ridges when piped and underfolding may lead to a very hollow shell. To test, drop a generous dollop of batter from the spatula. If it settles a little, but still holds a peak, it is time to stop folding.

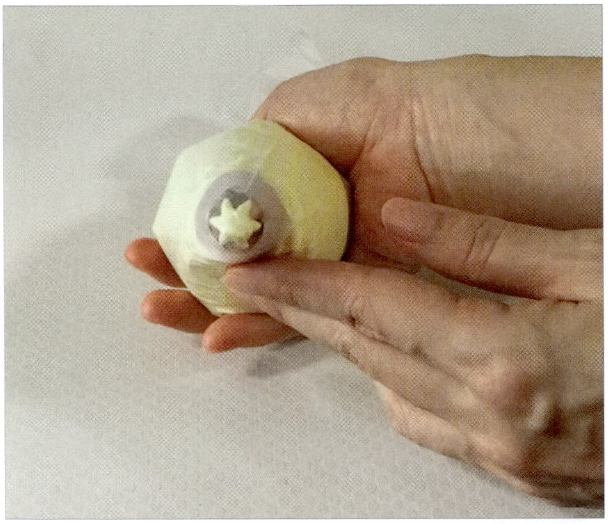

5. Transfer batter to a piping bag fitted with a 1-cm open star piping tip.

6. Pipe rosettes. Start piping from the middle.

7. And move the piping tip slowly outwards to form a swirl.

8. Hit tray just once to release any trapped air bubbles. The ridges will flatten out if you hit it too many times.

9. Let shells dry (page 24).

   NOTE It is trickier to be certain of when the shells are completely dry as the ridges dry faster than the valleys. Do check that the valleys are completely dry before baking.

10. Preheat oven to 160°C. Place tray on bottom or second lowest rack in oven, and bake for 5 minutes. Reduce oven temperature to 130°C and bake for 7–8 minutes, then reduce to 110°C and bake for a final 10 minutes or until feet do not appear wet.

11. Rotate tray halfway through baking. Let shells cool on tray before removing.

12. Prepare and pipe filling.

13. Store in an airtight container and refrigerate for at least 24 hours before serving.

Creating Swirl Patterns

Festive Lollipop Macarons

French Meringue Method

Makes 14–16 macarons

Scan the QR code to view a video tutorial on piping swirls.

75 g almond powder

75 g icing sugar

$^1/_8$ tsp salt

French Meringue

60 g egg whites, at room temperature

54 g castor sugar

$^1/_8$ tsp cream of tartar (optional)

Red, green and white gel food colouring

Suggested Filling

Vanilla or peppermint white chocolate (page 35)

1. Prepare baking tray and 4-cm circle template (page 95).
2. Sift together almond powder, icing sugar and salt. Set aside.
3. Prepare French meringue (page 16).
4. Prepare macaron batter (page 16). When the powdered ingredients are just incorporated, divide batter into 3 portions in the ratio 1 (red) : 1 (green) : 2 (white).
5. Add a little of the respective gel food colouring to each portion and fold in using a spatula.

6. Continue folding and pressing the batter against the side of the bowl until the right consistency is achieved (page 21).

7. Prepare the batter for the two-coloured swirls.
8. For the red and white swirl: lay a sheet of plastic wrap (A4 size) on your worktop. Carefully pour half the red batter, in a line, down the middle of the plastic wrap. Repeat using a third of the white batter.
9. For the green and white swirl: lay a sheet of plastic wrap (A4 size) on your worktop. Carefully pour half the green batter, in a line, down the middle of the plastic wrap. Repeat using a third of the white batter.

10. Prepare the batter for the three-coloured swirl.
11. Lay a third sheet of plastic wrap (A4 size) on your worktop. Carefully pour the remaining red batter in a line, down the middle of the plastic wrap, followed by the remaining green and white batters.

12. Wrap each set of batter up by bringing the long ends together to enclose the batter, then twisting both ends of the plastic wrap.
13. Use sticky tape to secure one of the twisted ends. This is to prevent the batter from leaking out from the top of the piping bag when piping.

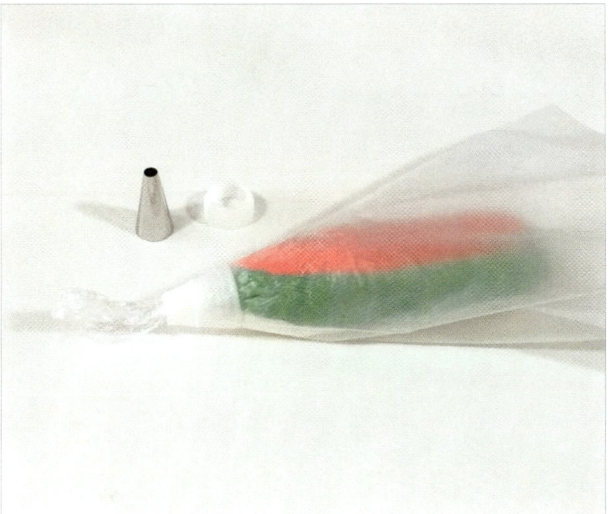

14. Pull the twisted end without tape through a piping bag fitted with a tip adapter.
15. Cut the twisted end of the cling wrap, then attach a 5–6-mm round tip.

16. Hold the piping tip perpendicular to the baking tray, about 5–7 mm away from the middle of a circle.
17. Apply pressure to the piping bag to pipe out a little batter. Release pressure and rotate the piping bag, taking care not to shift the position of the piping tip away from the centre of the circle by too much. Repeat applying pressure, releasing and rotating the piping bag until the batter is 2–3-mm away from the outline.
18. Hit tray on worktop to release any trapped air bubbles.
19. Let shells dry (page 24).

20. Preheat oven to 150°C. Place tray on bottom or second lowest rack in oven, and bake for 10 minutes. Reduce oven temperature to 130°C and bake for 5–10 minutes or until feet do not appear wet.
21. Rotate tray halfway through baking. Let shells cool on tray before removing.
22. Prepare filling. Pipe filling on a shell, place a cakepop stick in the middle and sandwich with another shell.
23. Store in an airtight container for at least 24 hours before serving.

Piping Batters Side-by-Side

Lunar New Year Macarons

Italian Meringue Method

Makes 40–50 macarons

Mass

200 g almond powder

200 g icing sugar

1/8 tsp salt (optional)

80 g egg whites, at room temperature

Orange/peach, red and black gel food colouring

1 tsp charcoal powder, sifted

Italian Meringue

80 g egg whites, at room temperature

200 g castor sugar

75 g water

1/8 tsp cream of tartar (optional)

Finishing

Black edible food marker

Peach-coloured lustre dust

Red sugar flowers

Flooding consistency yellow royal icing (page 28)

Suggested Filling

Strawberry SMBC (page 33) or strawberry white chocolate buttercream (page 34)

1. Prepare baking tray and Lunar New Year template (page 95).
2. Prepare mass. Sift together almond powder, icing sugar and salt. Add egg whites and mix well.
3. Divide mass into 3 portions in the ratio 1 (black) : 2 (beige) : 5 (red). Add a little of the respective gel food colouring to each portion and fold in using a spatula. Add charcoal powder to the black mass and mix well.
4. Prepare Italian meringue (page 20). Portion the meringue for each mass; each portion should be half the weight of the respective mass.

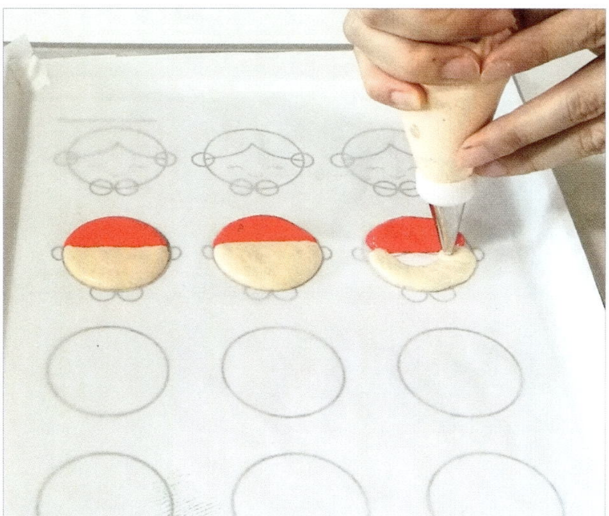

5. Prepare macaron batter (page 21). Fold meringue into mass.
6. Transfer each batter to a piping bag fitted with a 4–5-mm round tip.

   Using the trace-and-fill technique (page 50), pipe a semi-circle using the red batter for the boy's cap and another semi-circle using the beige batter for the boy's face. Use a toothpick to nudge the batter to fill the shape.

7. Using the same technique, pipe the girl's hair using the black batter and her face using the beige batter. Use a toothpick to nudge the batter to fill the shape.
8. Hit tray on worktop to release any trapped air bubbles.
9. Set aside for 15 minutes or until a thin membrane is formed.

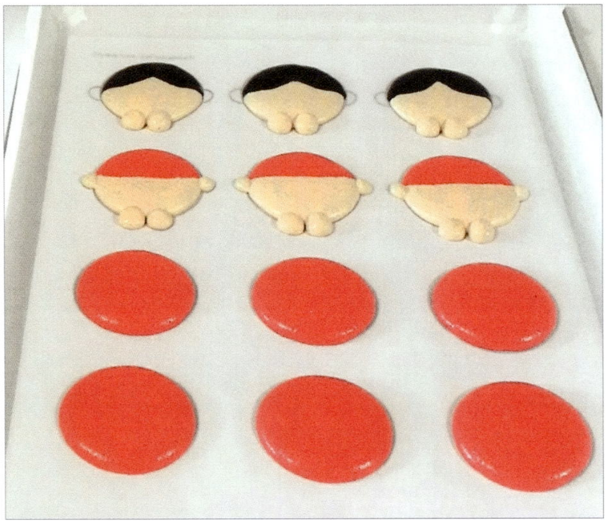

10. Using the beige batter, pipe two small circles for hands for both boy and girl, and ears for the boy.

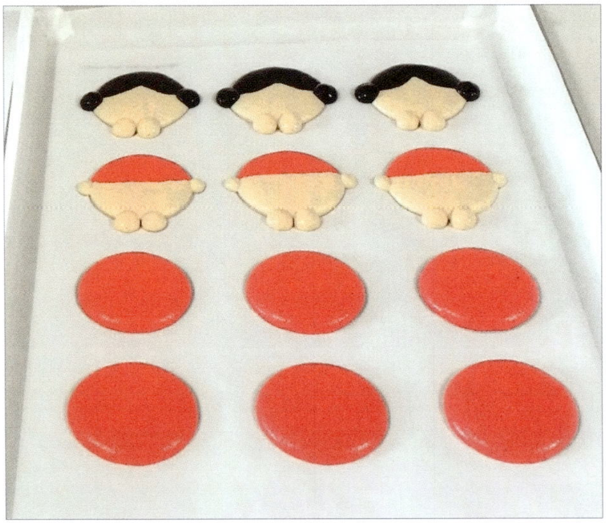

11. Using the black batter, pipe buns for the girl.
12. Gently tap the bottom of the tray to release any trapped air bubbles, being careful not to disturb the segments that were piped earlier.
13. Let shells dry (page 24).
14. Preheat oven to 140°C. Place tray on bottom or second lowest rack in oven, and bake for 10 minutes, then reduce oven temperature to 130°C and bake for 5–10 minutes or until feet do not appear wet.
15. Rotate tray halfway through baking. Let shells cool on tray before removing.

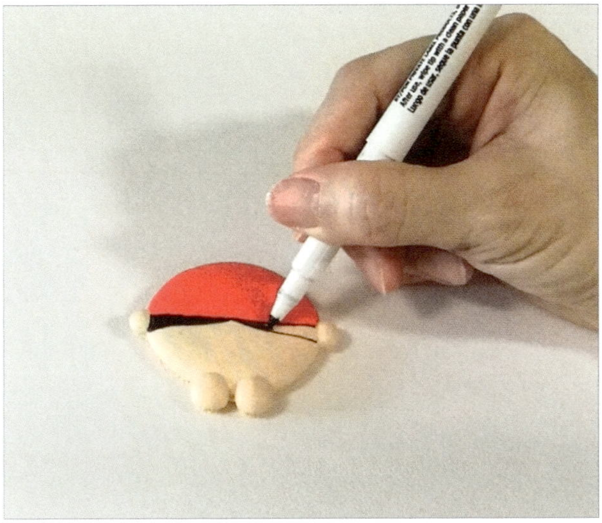

16. Draw eyes and mouth of boy and girl using black edible food marker. Draw hair for boy.
17. Using a small dry brush, dab a little lustre dust for the cheeks.

18. Pipe designs on boy's cap using yellow royal icing. Use a toothpick to nudge the icing into place.

19. Glue red sugar flowers on the girl's head using royal icing. Set aside to dry for an hour.
20. Prepare and pipe filling.
21. Store in an airtight container and refrigerate for at least 24 hours before serving.

Creating Hemispherical Shells

Hedgehog Macarons

Italian Meringue Method

Makes 25–45 macarons

Mass

200 g almond powder

200 g icing sugar

1/8 tsp salt (optional)

80 g egg whites, at room temperature

14 g cocoa powder, sifted

Orange/peach gel food colouring

Italian Meringue

80 g egg whites, at room temperature

200 g castor sugar

75 g water

1/8 tsp cream of tartar (optional)

Finishing

Medium consistency black royal icing (page 28)

Suggested Filling

Dark chocolate ganache (page 31)

Raspberry jam (page 32)

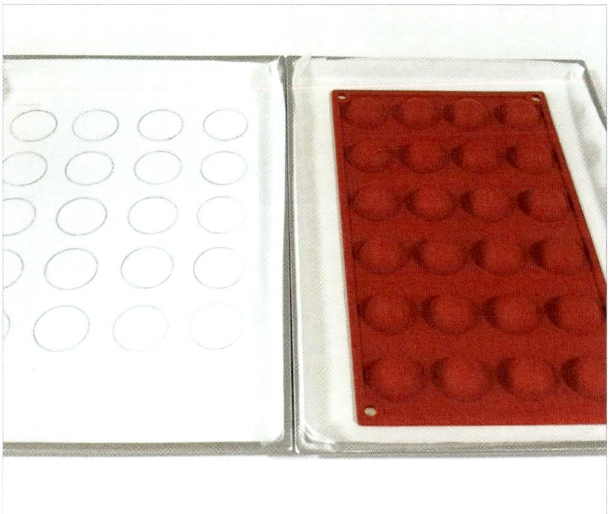

1. Prepare baking tray and circle template (page 89). Prepare another baking tray and place a silicone cake pop mould upside down on the tray. There should be sufficient space for the mould to expand during baking.

   NOTE The size of the circle template should be slightly larger than the diameter of the cavities in your silicone cake pop mould. I use a 3.5-cm circle template for 3-cm cavities.

2. Prepare mass. Sift together almond powder, icing sugar and salt. Add egg whites and mix well.
3. Divide mass into 2 portions in the ratio 3 (brown) : (1) beige. Add cocoa powder to the bigger portion and a little orange/peach gel food colouring to the smaller portion and mix well.

4. Prepare Italian meringue (page 20). Portion the meringue for each mass; each portion should be half the weight of the respective mass.
5. Prepare macaron batter (page 21). Fold meringue into mass.
6. Transfer each batter into a piping bag fitted with a 4-mm round tip.
7. Pipe circles using brown batter.
8. Hit tray on worktop to release any trapped air bubbles.

9. Pipe hemispherical shells on the mounds of the overturned cake pop mould. Start by piping batter on the rough positions of the face and body. Do not pipe to cover the mounds as the batter will flow downwards naturally.
10. Use a toothpick to nudge the batter downwards to cover the mound.

    NOTE It is tricky to know how much batter to pipe, but you will get the hang of it with practise. You can always add more batter if there is not enough.

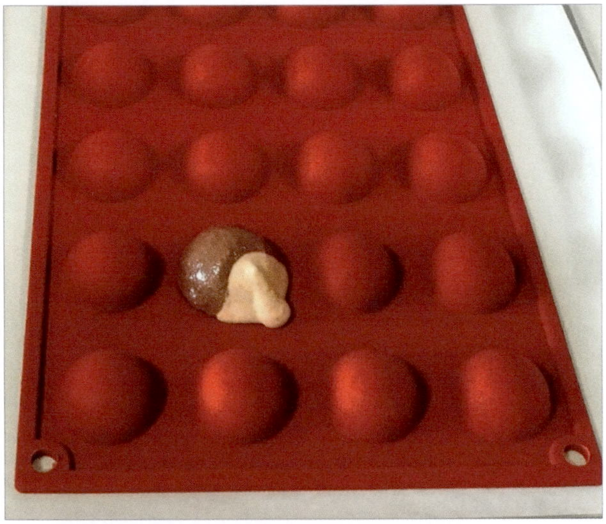

11. Pipe a little blob of beige batter for the snout and use a toothpick to smoothen it out.

12. Use a toothpick to pull the dark brown batter towards the beige batter for the spikes around the hedgehog's face.
13. Let dry for about 15 minutes or until a sticky membrane is formed.

14. Pipe spikes all over the body using brown batter.
15. Pipe ears using beige batter.
16. Let shells dry (page 24).

17. Preheat oven to 140°C. Place circles on bottom or second lowest rack in oven, and bake for 10 minutes, then reduce oven temperature to 130°C and bake for 5–10 minutes or until feet do not appear wet.
18. Bring oven back to 140°C and bake hemispherical shells for 10 minutes, then reduce temperature to 110°C and bake for another 30 minutes to 1 hour, if necessary, or until feet do not appear wet.
19. Let shells cool on tray before removing.

    NOTE Thoroughly baked shells should be fairly easy to remove from the mould. Don't worry about overbaking. Simply let the shells mature for a longer time after they are filled, or brush the inner surface with syrup or cream before filling.

20. Pipe eyes and nose using black royal icing.
21. Prepare filling.
22. Turn hemispherical shells over and sit them in the cavities of the cake pop mould to keep them steady as you work.
23. Coat the insides with a layer of dark chocolate ganache, then fill the centre with jam. Cover jam with more dark chocolate ganache.
24. Enclose filling using the round shells, then turn hedgehogs right side up.
25. Store in an airtight container and refrigerate for at least 24 hours before serving.

Assembling Macaron Structures

Unicorn Macaron Carousel

Italian Meringue Method

Makes one large macaron structure

Macaron Carousel

5 unicorn macarons (page 50)
One 13-cm macaron (page 36)
One 6-cm macaron (page 36)
Two 3.5-cm macarons (page 36)
One scalloped circle (page 58)
One 3.5-cm macaron shell (page 36)
Six 2.5-cm macaron shells (page 36)

Assembly Materials

5 paper straws
One 15-cm round cakeboard
Stiff consistency white royal icing (page 28)

Filling

Strawberry white chocolate (page 35)

1. Mount unicorns on paper straws. Pipe some strawberry white chocolate on the bottom shells of unicorns. Place paper straw in the middle of unicorns, such that the bottom end of the straw is about 2.5-cm away from the belly. Pipe more strawberry white chocolate to cover straw. Sandwich with top shell.
2. Place in an airtight container at room temperature and set aside for several hours or overnight for filling to set before assembling on carousel.

3. Assemble central pillar. Spoon royal icing into a piping bag fitted with a small open star piping tip. Pipe a little royal icing in the middle of the cakeboard and place the 13-cm macaron on it. Press down gently but firmly.
4. Pipe some royal icing in the middle of the 13-cm macaron and press the 6-cm macaron on it.
5. Pipe some royal icing in the middle of the 6-cm macaron and press the 3.5-cm macaron on it.
6. Pipe some royal icing in the middle of the 3.5-cm macaron and press another 3.5-cm macaron on it.
7. Set aside to dry for at least an hour.

8. Assemble roof. Pipe some strawberry white chocolate in the middle of the scalloped roof and press a 3.5-cm macaron shell on it.
9. Pipe some strawberry white chocolate in the middle of the 3.5-cm macaron shell and press a 2.5-cm macaron shell on it.
10. Pipe a decorative dollop of royal icing on top of the 2.5-cm shell.

11. Pipe some royal icing on top of the 3.5-cm macaron on the central pillar and place the roof over it, making sure it is in line with the pillar. Set aside for 15 minutes.

12. Stand the unicorns on the 13-cm macaron and trim the top of the paper straw so it just reaches the roof of the carousel.

13. To mount the unicorns on the caousel, pipe a swirl of royal icing on the 13-cm macaron and some icing on the roof directly above it. Carefully attach the base and top of the straw onto the carousel frame.

14. Count about three and a quarter segments on the carousel roof and position the next straw there.
15. Repeat until all the unicorns are mounted on the frame.

16. Pipe a little icing at the top end of each straw and attach a 2.5-cm macaron shell on it.
17. Leave the structure to dry for an hour before moving it.
18. Store at cool room temperature for 5 days or up to 2 weeks in the refrigerator.

Troubleshooting Guide

Shells have browned on the outside, but are still wet inside

Your oven temperature could be set too high. Use an oven thermometer to check the temperature of your oven to ensure the temperature setting is accurate. You can also try placing the baking tray on the lowest rack in the oven or turning the temperature down and baking for a longer time after the initial 16–20 minutes.

The macaron shells appear patchy

The patches on the shells are actually due to the oil that seeped out of the almond powder. To prevent this from happening, always store almond powder in the refrigerator in an airtight container or resealable bag. If the macarons still turn out patchy, dry out that batch of almond powder before using again. To do this, spread the almond powder out in a thin layer on a baking tray lined with paper towels. Bake in an oven at 90°C for 30 minutes, then let cool completely before sifting with icing sugar.

The batter turned bubbly after sitting out for a while

This is a sign of the meringue breaking down. For the French method, this is due to an underbeaten meringue. For the Italian method, either the egg whites were underbeaten or the meringue was not beaten long enough until it was cool after the syrup was added.

The Italian meringue batter is runny even after folding until no traces of meringue is seen

Chances are the egg whites were not beaten to the correct soft peak stage before the syrup was added. The batter can still be used, but the piped batter will take a long time to dry.

The baked macaron shells are hollow

This is probably the most common problem encountered by home bakers. A combination of factors can cause this:

The oven temperature was too low during the initial baking time before the internal structure could set. The oven temperature has to be between 130°C and 140°C during the initial 10–15 minutes of baking time (depending on the size of the macarons and the meringue used). Use an oven thermometer to monitor the oven temperature while baking.

The shells are underbaked, therefore their internal structure is not fully set. So when the shells are removed from the oven, they collapse internally. Reduce the oven temperature towards the second half of the baking time to ensure the shells are baked through but not browned.

The meringue was not beaten to the correct stiff peak stage. Underbeaten meringue will have peaks that curl a little at the end and overbeaten meringue will look lumpy or broken.

For the Italian method, the egg whites were not beaten to soft peaks before the syrup was added. Check that the egg whites are able to hold a peak for a second before disappearing and the egg white bubbles are fine in size.

The Italian meringue not beaten long enough until it was cool. Make sure that the meringue is sufficiently cooled before you stop beating at high speed. This make take 10–15 minutes depending on the size of the recipe. I usually have a fan blowing at the stand mixer to help the meringue cool more quickly. The meringue should at least be at body temperature before you stop beating.

There were trapped air bubbles in the batter. These will gather to form a large air pocket under the outermost layer of the shell. Tap the tray hard on the table top several times to release any trapped air bubbles before leaving the pipe batter to air-dry.

The batter was under-folded. This applies to both the French and Italian methods. Not enough air was knocked out of the batter when folding. Use the fold and press technique when mixing the macaron batter to knock the air out of the meringue. Be careful not to over-mix either as over-mixed batter will be runny. Test the consistency of the batter often.

Design Templates

Use these templates to guide you in piping the macarons. Make a photocopy of your chosen design and enlarge it by 200%. Place the template on the baking tray and place a sheet of baking paper over it before piping. The template can be kept and reused each time you bake.

Piping Circles (page 36)
2.5-cm circles (Enlarge 200%)

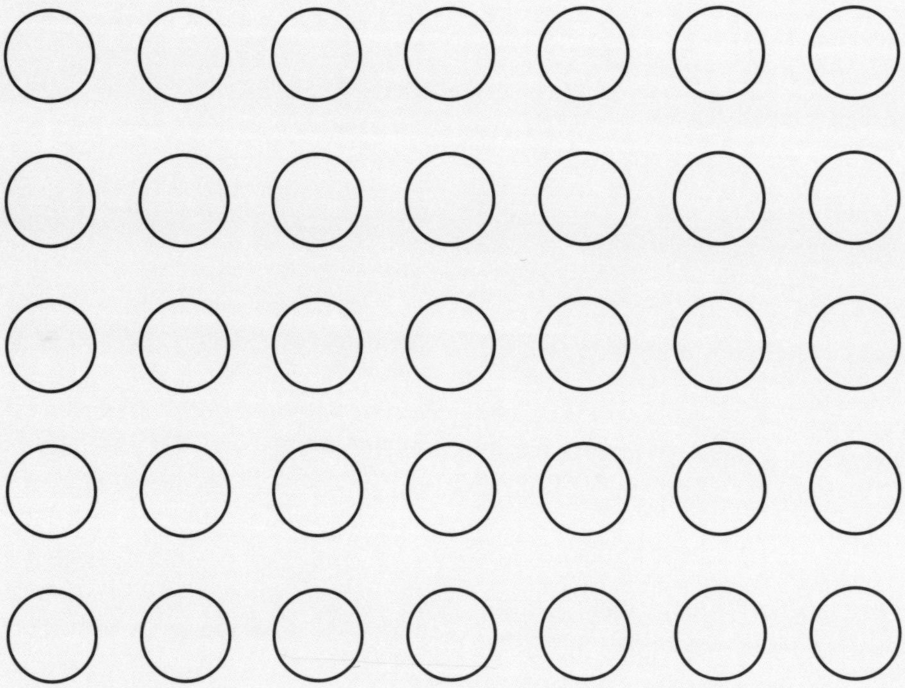

Piping Circles (page 36)
3.5-cm circles (Enlarge 200%)

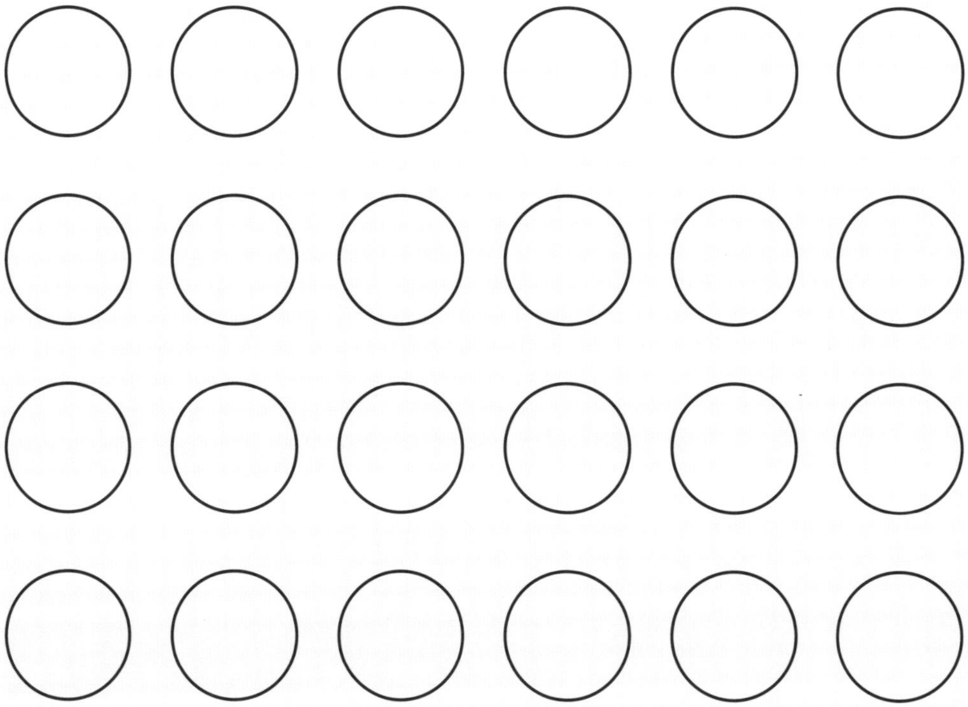

Piping Circles (page 36)
6-cm circles (Enlarge 200%)

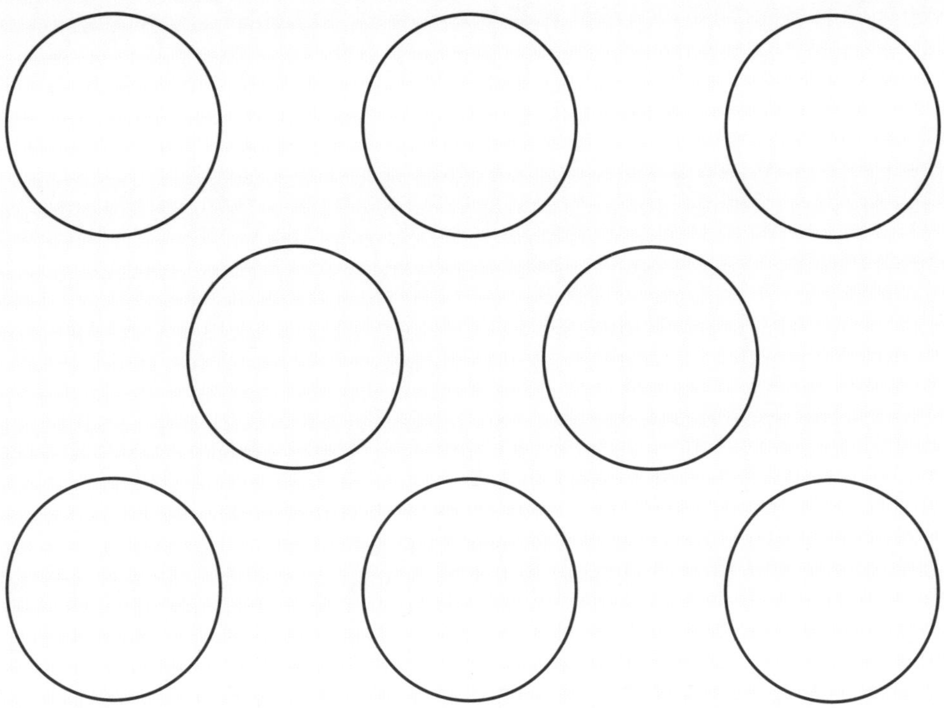

Piping Circles (page 36)

13-cm circles (Enlarge 200%)

Piping Hearts (page 40)

Pastel Heart Macarons (Enlarge 200%)

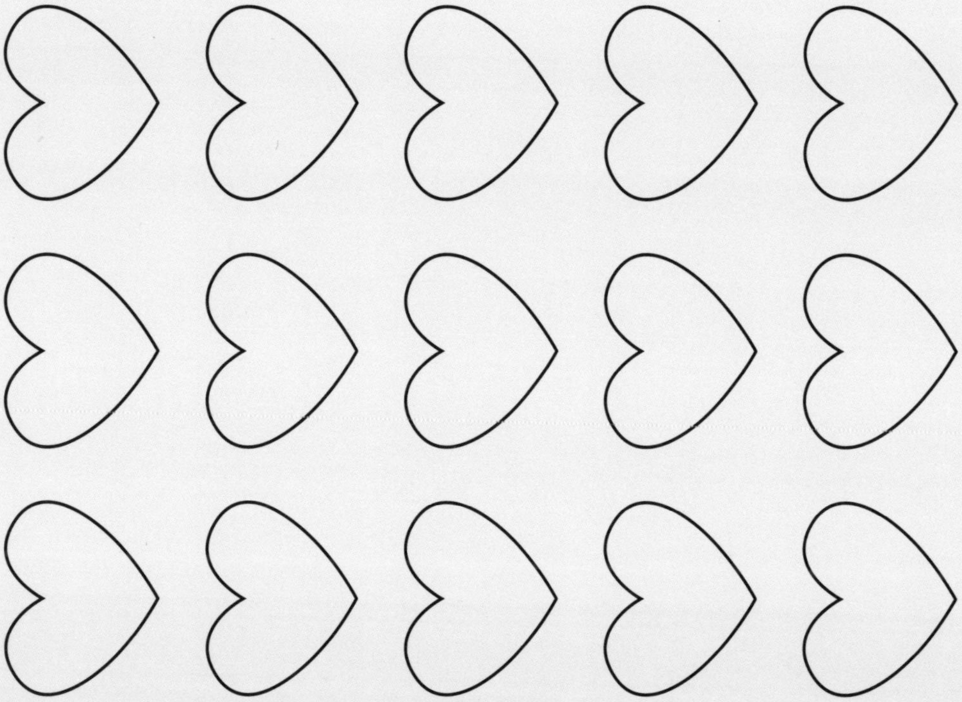

Piping Squares (page 44)

Mortarboard Macarons (Enlarge 200%)

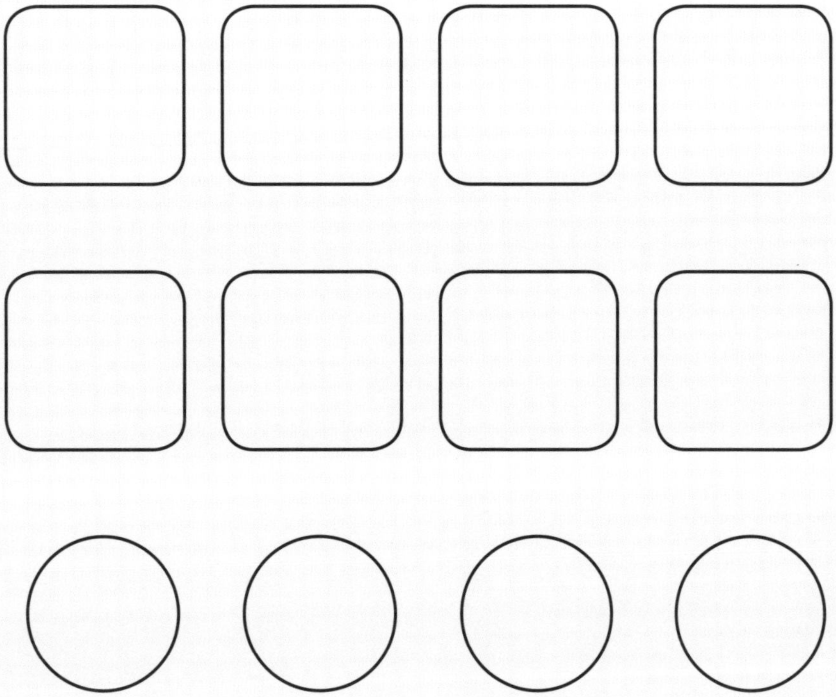

Piping Triangles (page 46)

Snow-capped Mountain Macarons (Enlarge 200%)

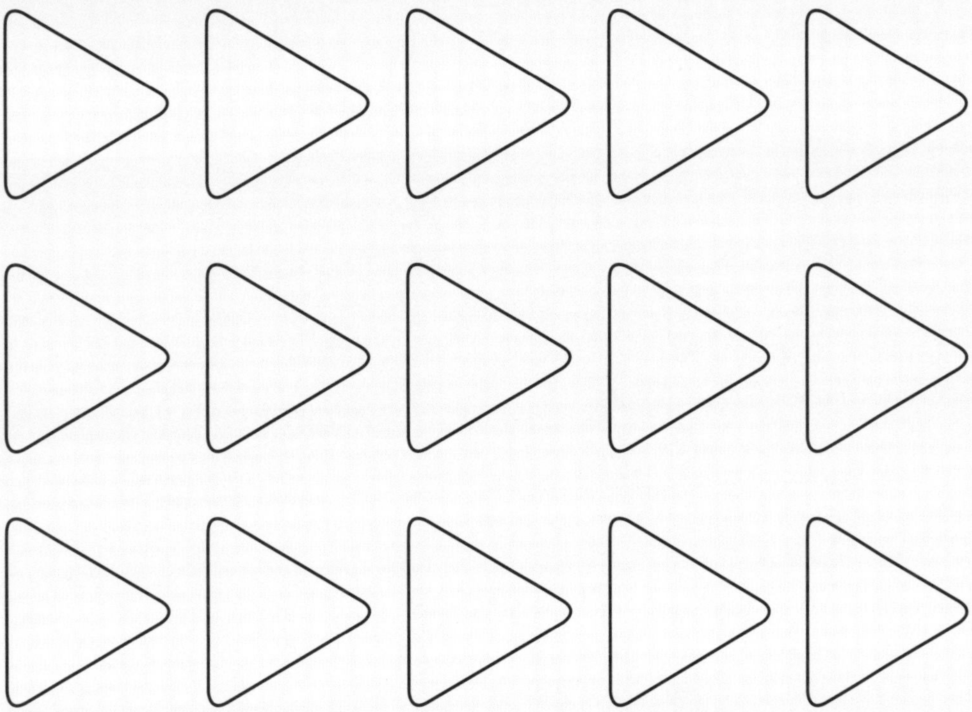

Creating Fine Features (page 48)

Baby Chick Macarons (Enlarge 200%)

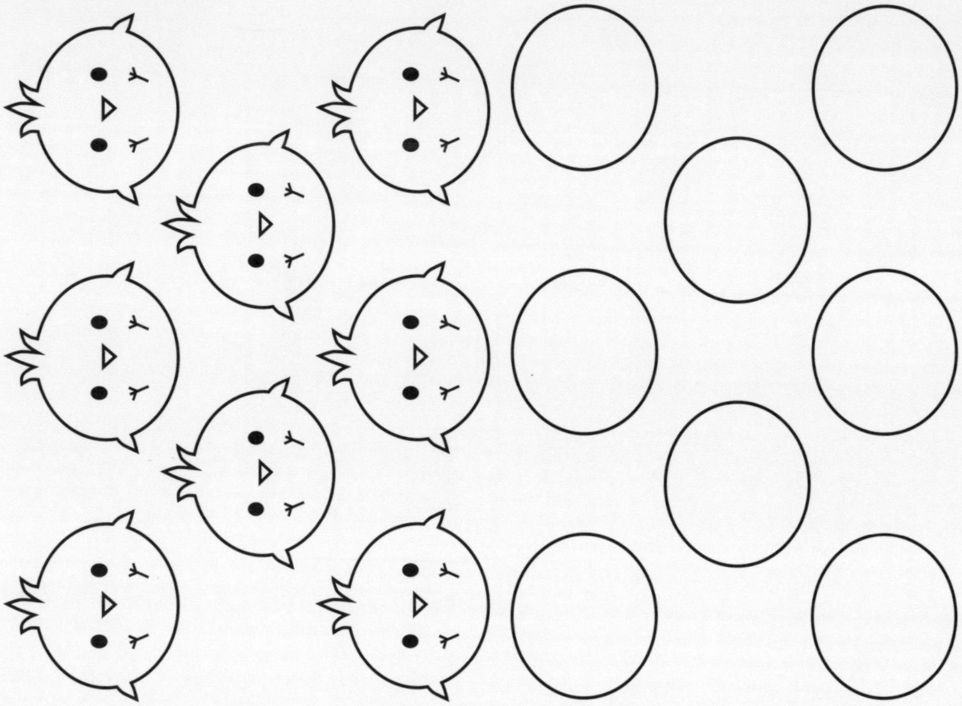

Creating Complex Shapes (page 50)

Trace-and-Fill Technique, Unicorn Macarons (Enlarge 200%)

Creating Pop-up Features (page 54)

Rose Macarons (Enlarge 200%)

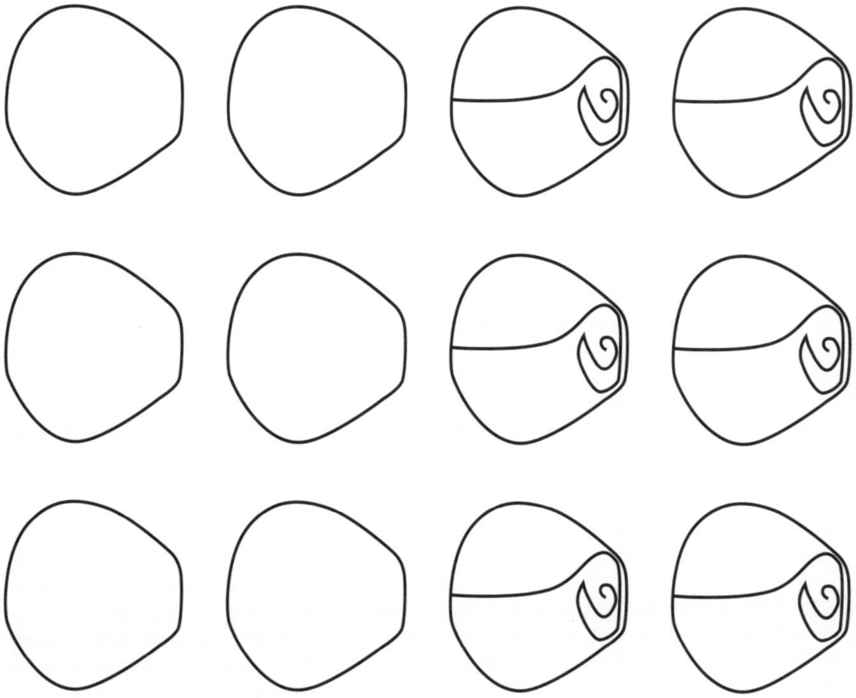

Creating Definition (page 58)

Scalloped Circle Macarons (Enlarge 200%)

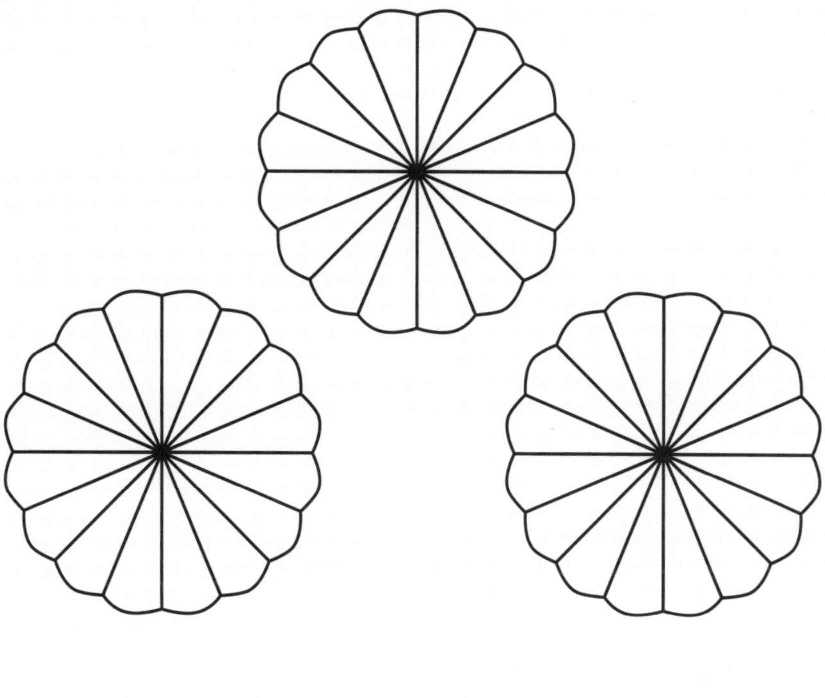

Creating Indented Features (page 62)

Happy Hippo Macarons (Enlarge 200%)

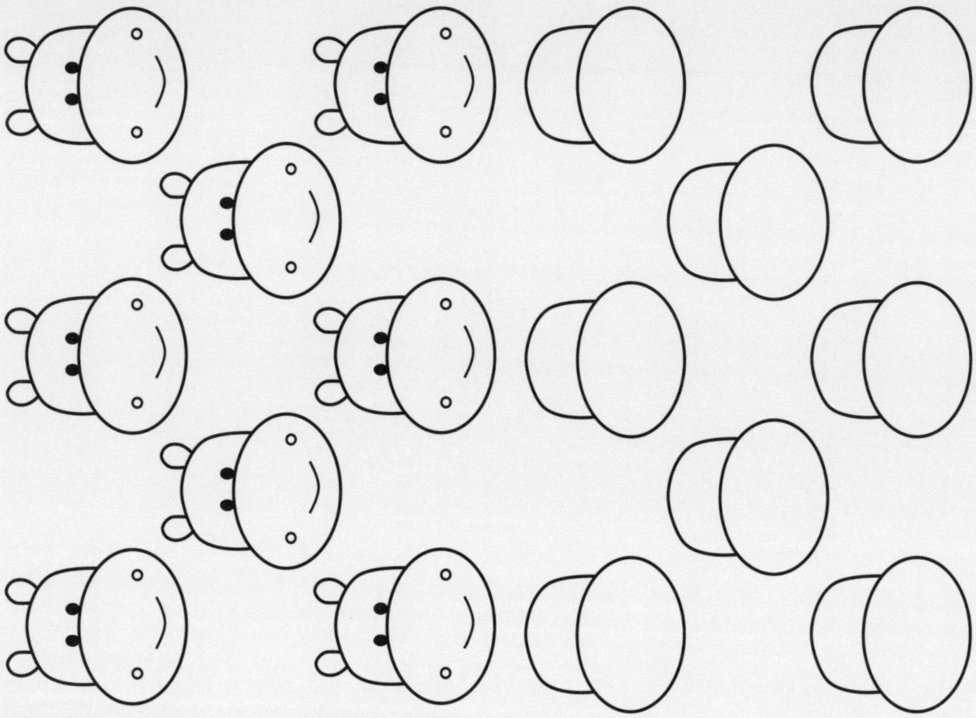

Creating Raised Smooth Features (page 66)

Rosette Macarons, 5-cm circles (Enlarge 200%)

Creating Swirl Patterns (page 70)

Festive Lollipop Macarons, 4-cm circles (Enlarge 200%)

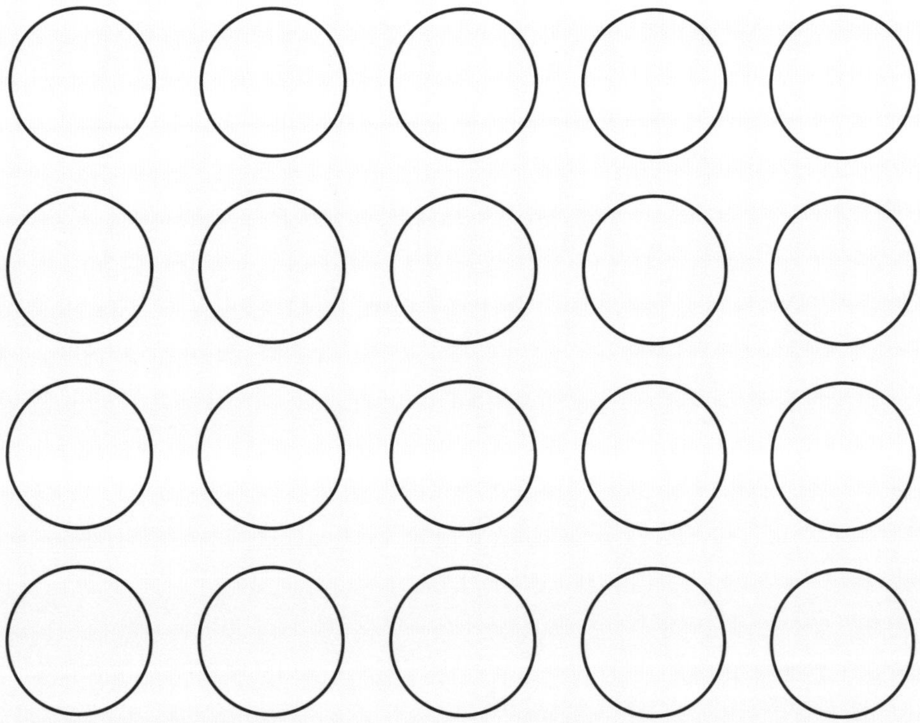

Piping Batters Side-by-Side (page 74)

Lunar New Year Macarons (Enlarge 200%)

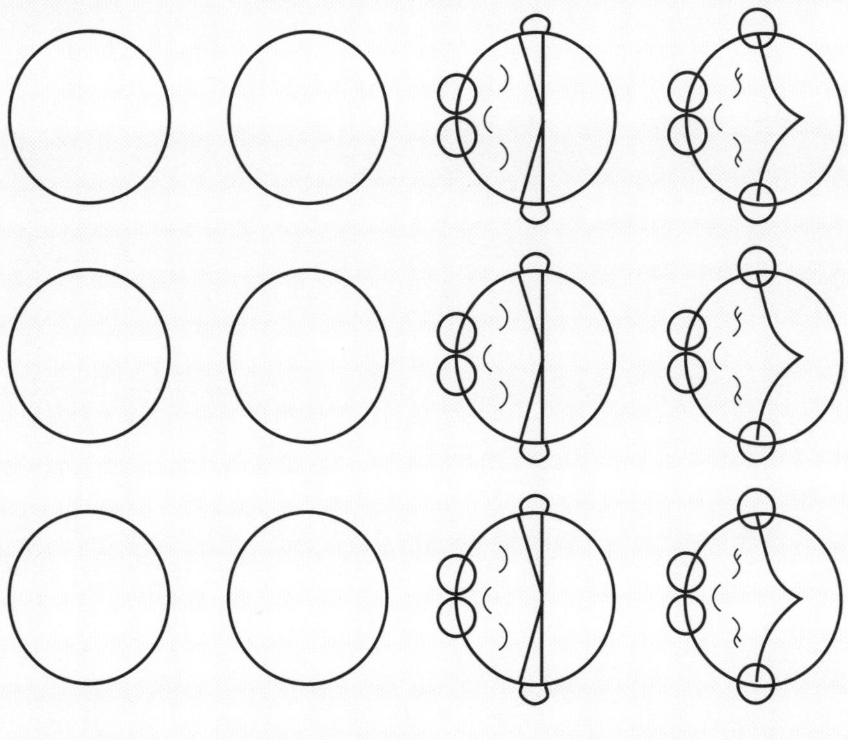

Weights & Measures

Quantities for this book are given in metric and American (spoon) measures. Standard spoon measurements used are: 1 teaspoon = 5 ml and 1 tablespoon = 15 ml. All measures are level unless otherwise stated.

LIQUID AND VOLUME MEASURES

Metric	Imperial	American
5 ml	1/6 fl oz	1 teaspoon
10 ml	1/3 fl oz	1 dessertspoon
15 ml	1/2 fl oz	1 tablespoon
60 ml	2 fl oz	1/4 cup (4 tablespoons)
85 ml	2 1/2 fl oz	1/3 cup
90 ml	3 fl oz	3/8 cup (6 tablespoons)
125 ml	4 fl oz	1/2 cup
180 ml	6 fl oz	3/4 cup
250 ml	8 fl oz	1 cup
300 ml	10 fl oz (1/2 pint)	1 1/4 cups
375 ml	12 fl oz	1 1/2 cups
435 ml	14 fl oz	1 3/4 cups
500 ml	16 fl oz	2 cups
625 ml	20 fl oz (1 pint)	2 1/2 cups
750 ml	24 fl oz (1 1/5 pints)	3 cups
1 litre	32 fl oz (1 3/5 pints)	4 cups
1.25 litres	40 fl oz (2 pints)	5 cups
1.5 litres	48 fl oz (2 2/5 pints)	6 cups
2.5 litres	80 fl oz (4 pints)	10 cups

OVEN TEMPERATURE

	°C	°F	Gas Regulo
Very slow	120	250	1
Slow	150	300	2
Moderately slow	160	325	3
Moderate	180	350	4
Moderately hot	190/200	370/400	5/6
Hot	210/220	410/440	6/7
Very hot	230	450	8
Super hot	250/290	475/550	9/10

DRY MEASURES

Metric	Imperial
30 grams	1 ounce
45 grams	1 1/2 ounces
55 grams	2 ounces
70 grams	2 1/2 ounces
85 grams	3 ounces
100 grams	3 1/2 ounces
110 grams	4 ounces
125 grams	4 1/2 ounces
140 grams	5 ounces
280 grams	10 ounces
450 grams	16 ounces (1 pound)
500 grams	1 pound, 1 1/2 ounces
700 grams	1 1/2 pounds
800 grams	1 3/4 pounds
1 kilogram	2 pounds, 3 ounces
1.5 kilograms	3 pounds, 4 1/2 ounces
2 kilograms	4 pounds, 6 ounces

LENGTH

Metric	Imperial
0.5 cm	1/4 inch
1 cm	1/2 inch
1.5 cm	3/4 inch
2.5 cm	1 inch

ABBREVIATION

tsp	teaspoon
Tbsp	tablespoon
g	gram
kg	kilogram
ml	millilitre